are to be returned on or before
the last date below.

D1583620

Hope Springs

RICHARD CONLON

Activities by **Mike Gould**

Heinemann Educational Publishers
Halley Court, Jordan Hill, Oxford OX2 8EJ
Part of Harcourt Education

Heinemann is a registered trademark of
Harcourt Education Limited

First published 2006

10 09 08 07 06
10 9 8 7 6 5 4 3 2 1

British Library Cataloguing in Publication Data
is available from the British Library on request.

10-digit ISBN: 0 435 9999 66
13-digit ISBN: 978 0 435 999 96 4

Editorial: Louise Curphey, Hilary Fine
Design: Phil Leafe
Typeset by Thomson Digital, India
Cover design by Forepoint
Printed in China by CTPS

Cover photo: © Alamy

Acknowledgements
Every effort has been made to contact
copyright holders of material reproduced in
this book. Any omissions will be rectified in
subsequent printings if notice is given to the
publishers.

Contents

Author's notes

Hope Springs was originally written to be performed seamlessly, with the exception of the interval. The numbered scenes have been inserted to assist with making it work as a piece for reading in the classroom. They occur at moments that seemed to make a sort of sense to me, but in performance one has always run naturally into the other.

The text is gender-neutral throughout and can be approached by casts of either gender or any mix of both. Needless to say, casting throws up an interesting debate about gender politics and can shine new light on the lines. I hope this approach to writing the play means teachers can give the most appropriate part to the most suitable pupil.

Familiarity with the characters of the Pupils will give readers and performers a chance to inhabit them and find a way to deliver lines that works. For ease of use, though, I make the suggestions in the Cast List by way of a few clues.

Cast List

Ringleader, *intelligent, charming and charismatic; quick to anger and quick to cool.*

Inspector, *has a natural authority; observant with keen judgement.*

Assistant, *a little slow witted, but not a buffoon.*

Principal, *brisk, cold and businesslike, but should not be played as evil or malevolent.*

Sam, *sensitive and thoughtful; prone to melancholy.*

Pupil 1, *used to getting what they want through their looks and charm – a flirt*

Pupil 2, *street-wise and assured; cocky, almost to the point of aggression*

Pupil 3, *idealistic, principled and thoughtful*

Pupil 4, *mercurial, creative, sardonic*

Pupil 5, *a thief and a liar, with an aggression just barely below the surface*

Pupil 6, *nervous and twitchy, with a record of fire-setting*

Pupil 7, *bewildered and unnerved; borderline learning disability*

Pupil 8, *anxious and timid; a conflict avoider, keen to go unnoticed*

Pupil 9, *not afraid to speak their own mind, but can be devious; eager to please whoever is of most use*

Pupil 10, *indignant and impulsive, with more than a hint of truculence*

Parents, *should not be shown to be monsters, they need to seem to have few options left.*

Staff, *manipulative and divisive.*

Island Voices, *the chorus (comprising a minimum of six people); they can slip in and out of being observers, scene-setters and characters in their own right*

A version of *Hope Springs* was first performed in 2004 by IMPACT at The Castle Theatre, Wellingborough.

Act One

Scene 1

During the opening section, each strand (the letter, Island voices, Parents, Principal, Pupils and Staff) is totally unconnected to the others; there should be no confusion that they are referring to each other. They should occupy separate areas of the stage. As the house lights fade, the Island voices can be heard.

ISLAND VOICES (*suggesting an attempt to calm or quiet someone while also recalling the sound of the sea*)
Shh … Shh … Shh …

The Ringleader stands alone, unfolds a piece of paper and begins to silently read.

SAM To all my friends … This is not an easy letter to write. I'm going to miss all of you more than many of you think. There's no point in me pretending that my time here has   5
been happy – I don't think any of us can say that, but many of you have made it … as bearable as it ever could be …

All of the Island voices instructions throughout the play ('Insert disc', 'Play', etc.) should be neutral and crisp.

ISLAND VOICES 'Hope Springs.'

ISLAND VOICES **1** On-Screen Promotional Brochure.   10
AND **2**

3

ISLAND VOICES **3** AND **4**	National Parent Market.
ISLAND VOICES **5** AND **6**	Insert disc.
ISLAND VOICES	Play.

Music. The Principal appears, as if in an advert for the facility. The Principal can move around the stage without intruding on any other characters.

PRINCIPAL   Welcome to Hope Springs. As you can see, our institution is nestled in a beautiful, rugged 15 island landscape, only accessible by boat. Over the years, word has spread about the work we do here. Whatever you may have heard, take this from me: we get results – the results that you want. 20

ISLAND VOICES   Stop.

PUPIL **1**   (*indignantly*) I couldn't believe it. I never thought they would do this. Who doesn't go through some kind of dodgy period, for god's sake? I'm young, I'm supposed 25 to be having fun. My parents thought I would be this person who was going to be all-virginal and pure until I was in a serious relationship, then give myself completely when I got married. I don't think so. Life's 30 too short for that isn't it?

Turning on the charm.

I want to enjoy myself a bit – but that doesn't make me evil does it? Look at me. You can

	tell I'm a nice person, can't you? I still can't
	believe they sent me here. 35
ALL PARENTS	You just can't imagine what it was like for us.
STAFF 1	Excuse me … just *what* do you think you're
	doing in here?
PRINCIPAL	So who are we? The staff and board of this
	facility work for a very successful company 40
	called Youth Correction Limited. We have a
	number of institutions across the country,
	all working towards the same goal: to save
	your son or your daughter.
ISLAND VOICES	Stop. 45
PUPIL 2	(*angry*) They think that even if you just
	experiment, it's going to get out of control
	and you'll end up as a junkie on the street.
	I wasn't doing anything most of my friends
	weren't doing. My parents drink wine every 50
	day, and that's a drug! But that's OK isn't it,
	because that's nice and middle class.
	They're the ones who are supposed to love
	me and care for me. How could they send
	me here? 55
ALL PARENTS	We just didn't know where to turn.
STAFF 2	Right, you are in such deep trouble.
PRINCIPAL	Facilities like Hope Springs have been thriving
	in the US for years. They work. They deal
	with the world as it is, not as we might 60
	want it to be. Ask yourself, can you really
	control that teenager who is on the edge
	of doing something unwise? What are their
	friends really like. Do you have to put up

	with a disrespectful child who may well 65
	be drinking and smoking and dabbling in
	drugs and sleeping around? Dealing with
	these issues is your responsibility, but we're
	on your side – sending a child to us is
	absolutely a sign of love. Just ask yourself, 70
	is your child safer on the streets with the
	pimps and drug-dealers and junkies, or
	here with us?

ISLAND VOICES Stop.

PUPIL 3 (*defiant*) We just didn't agree on anything;   75
we're on opposite sides on every issue. I've
realised that my parents are Nazis. Small-
minded bigots. All I ever did was go on
demonstrations, help organise rallies and
things. Yes, I got arrested – not because   80
I was breaking the law, but because the
police are Nazis too. My parents must be
fascists; only a fascist would have sent me
here.

ALL PARENTS We didn't feel that we had a choice.   85

STAFF 1 Now, now, come on. Don't be hasty …

PRINCIPAL So, you've heard of our reputation and now
you have decided to find out more. And
why? Because you care. And because the
option of doing nothing and hoping for   90
the best is for … well, not for parents who
truly love their children. Come with me
now, and we'll look at the buildings and
the wonderful remote setting which are
on offer to you, the concerned parents of   95
today's young people.

ISLAND VOICES	Stop.
PUPIL 4	(*quiet and intense*) I hated school, I mean really hated it. My parents had this dream that I'd go on to be a doctor or a lawyer or 100 something, but it's just not me. I'd rather work in a shop. I want to be in a band really, that's what I'd love. But they didn't get that. We'd have screaming rows. I'd almost have stand-up fights with my dad … me! 105 He wants me to be what he 'never had the chance to be', he says. Well I didn't fancy being made to succeed where he failed, thank you very much … but I never thought I'd end up here. 110
ALL PARENTS	We were worried sick.
STAFF 2	I mean it … don't do anything you might regret! Think about it!
PRINCIPAL	This old Victorian country house is both the educational centre, dormitories and 115 correctional facility. The staff live on site; your children are never alone. There is nowhere else to go, nowhere to run to. We own the island and every building on it. When you sign over 49 per cent of your 120 parental rights to our company, we become the only family and the only home they will need – until we get the results you want.
ISLAND VOICES	Stop.
PUPIL 5	(*aggressive*) If I lived with my dad, he 125 would have understood; he wasn't a saint when he was young. He'd have been cool about it. I didn't steal anything major – it was

just for the laugh, the buzz, because there
was nothing else to do where we lived. But   130
my step-dad, he's a self-made man, loaded
too. He hit me once, just once – so I
flattened him …

As if relishing the memory.

… laid him out. I still think I was right to, but I
wish I hadn't … enjoyed it … so much. So   135
she let him send me here.

ALL PARENTS   I'm asking you: what else were we supposed
to do?

STAFF **1** AND **2**   Please don't! No! Please … no!

ALL PARENTS   What else *could* we do?   140

PRINCIPAL   There are days when being the principal of
this institution can be hard. On those days I
take a few hours to myself and walk to
what I feel is a very special place indeed.
Here, nestled deep within the woods, far   145
from the main house, are the natural features
which give our facility its name. The water
that gushes from these rocks at the mouth
of this isolated cave was discovered by this
island's first settlers hundreds of years ago, 150
just as they were about to give up trying to
find a source of fresh water, and therefore
the chance to survive and thrive here.
They knew then that they had found a better
place. So these are the Hope Springs,   155
and here I sit and reflect when I need to
recharge my personal batteries, before I
rejoin the battle, the battle for the hearts

and minds of your children. It's not easy,
it's not attractive; our methods can, at first, 160
seem excessive, but they are necessary. I
believe, that with your help, this is a battle
we can win.

ALL PARENTS   We had to do something … It's absolutely a
sign of love.   165

PRINCIPAL   So, when things look bleak, when you are at
the end of your tether, remember – there is
a way forward. It's not hopeless; just when
you think there's nowhere to turn – Hope
Springs.   170

*The Ringleader crumples the letter and runs
offstage with great purpose.*

ISLAND VOICES   Stop. Rewind.

*Pupils, Parents and Staff exit. Sam, however,
should be a presence throughout the whole of
the first act.*

Scene 2

*Lights up on the Inspector and Assistant who
are clearly watching something on a screen.
Occasionally the Inspector flicks a remote
control at the screen to review sections of the
Principal's speech.*

INSPECTOR   Well, I must say, that's not an awful lot to
go on.

ASSISTANT   (*looks at the Inspector*) Is that it?

INSPECTOR_   That's it.   175

ASSISTANT	No report? No file?	
INSPECTOR	(*shakes head*) No.	
ASSISTANT	No pages and pages of evaluation?	
INSPECTOR	No.	
ASSISTANT	Well it looks … nice.	180
INSPECTOR	(*laughs and looks at the Assistant*) It's their publicity; of course they're going to make it look 'nice'.	
ISLAND VOICES	Play.	
PRINCIPAL	… *nestled in a beautiful, rugged island landscape, only accessible by boat* …	185
ISLAND VOICES	Forward.	
ASSISTANT	Aren't we supposed to have information on every school in the area?	
INSPECTOR	Perhaps you should stop thinking 'school' and start thinking 'correctional facility'.	190
ASSISTANT	Can't we go next week? Its hours away and I've got so much to do.	
INSPECTOR	(*authoritatively*) Someone needs to go out there and see that everything is in order. Apparently all communications are down, no one has heard a peep from them since last night, and so we're going to see that everything's OK. OK?	195
ASSISTANT	(*resigned*) OK.	200
INSPECTOR	Good.	
ISLAND VOICES	Play.	
PRINCIPAL	… *safer on the streets with the pimps and drug-dealers and junkies, or here* …	

ISLAND VOICES	Forward.	205
ASSISTANT	Can't the police go out there?	
INSPECTOR	It is hardly a job for the police.	
ASSISTANT	It's hardly a job for two educational inspectors.	
INSPECTOR	Excuse me? One educational inspector and one assistant.	210
ASSISTANT	OK. Fair point.	
INSPECTOR	So what we'll do is this – I'll inspect, and you'll assist.	
ASSISTANT	(*sighs*) OK. If we have to, we have to.	215
INSPECTOR	It will be interesting to have a look inside one of those places.	
ISLAND VOICES	Play.	
PRINCIPAL	*… when you sign over 49 per cent of your parental rights to our company …*	220
ISLAND VOICES	Forward.	
ASSISTANT	If they're on our patch, why don't we have a file on them? Why haven't we visited before?	
INSPECTOR	They're a private company; it's on private land, a private agreement between the parents and the organisation, a business arrangement. And not cheap either, so I believe. The laws that apply to these places are pretty new. Actually, it used to be illegal, but now, well now it's a bit of a grey area. So we leave them to it, unless we have a reason to drop in, which hasn't arisen until now.	225 230

ISLAND VOICES	Play.
PRINCIPAL	*… and walk to what I feel is a very special* 235 *place indeed …*
ISLAND VOICES	Forward.
ASSISTANT	We'll be gone all day I suppose?
INSPECTOR	An hour in the car, half an hour in a little boat.
ASSISTANT	(**looks pleased**) I like boats – I'm good in boats. 240
ISLAND VOICES	Play.
PRINCIPAL	*… they had found a better place …*
ISLAND VOICES	Stop. Eject.

The Principal exits. The Inspector and Assistant begin to put on coats, collect briefcases, etc.

INSPECTOR	It'll be interesting to meet this principal in person. With any luck we'll be there for 245 lunch; we'll have a look round and no doubt it'll just be some technical thing that's gone wrong – but still we will have a look, and you'll still be home for your tea.

Pats Assistant on the shoulder.

ASSISTANT	'Home for tea.' I like the sound of that. 250
INSPECTOR	One thing I am sure of is that these places are very smoothly and very efficiently run.

They exit.

Scene 3

Sudden noise of Pupils all talking at once.
As they spill on-stage, there is an argument

taking place. With just a physical gesture, the
Ringleader gradually makes the others quiet.

RINGLEADER   Thank you. Now … I think we can safely
say that, how can I put this, the old rules no
longer apply. We are under a new regime,   255
one of our own making, so we'd better try
and organise.

PUPIL 3   (*looking around*) I think that's fair enough.

PUPIL 9   This is crazy.

PUPIL 8   (*anxiously*) We're in so deep.   260

PUPIL 9   (*angrily*) You should never have done it.

PUPIL 8   Unwise, very unwise.

PUPIL 9   I didn't want any part of it.

PUPIL 7   I don't know what you're getting so worked
up about.   265

PUPIL 9   What …?!

The noise and argument begin again, but calms
as the Ringleader begins.

RINGLEADER   I think it's safe to assume that none of us
wanted anything to do with this place,
none of us wanted any part of it, but we
didn't really have a choice, did we? And   270
maybe what we've done is a little unwise, but
it was also unwise to just sit and take it.

PUPIL 2   (*as if in support*) Well I certainly couldn't
take it any more.

PUPIL 9   It's OK for you – you weren't progressing   275
like some of us were.

PUPIL 8   Yeah. You had less to lose.

PUPIL **9**	Some of us worked hard to move through this place.	
PUPIL **8**	Over a longer time than you've had.	280
PUPIL **9**	And now we'll be back where we started.	
PUPIL **3**	You call that progress?	
PUPIL **7**	Yeah … 'progress' …	
PUPIL **8**	It was our way out.	
RINGLEADER	I know you don't all like what we did, but it was hardly something we could have sat down and taken a vote on was it? It had to be done, and now we have to deal with how we carry on from here.	285
PUPIL **7**	(*anxiously*) Well I want to leave! I have to get away from this place. It's doing my head in, still being here.	290
RINGLEADER	You will.	
PUPIL **7**	Are you sure?	

The Ringleader walks to Pupil 7 and puts a hand on their shoulder.

RINGLEADER	One way or another, you *will* leave here.	295

To the whole group.

	But first, we have to get organised. We still need to eat; we still need to keep this place running like there's no change.	
PUPIL **2**	But everything's changed.	
PUPIL **10**	(*shouts*) I want to rip it down, brick by brick.	300
PUPIL **6**	(*looks at Pupil 10*) I want to torch it.	
PUPIL **3**	Don't start on that!	

RINGLEADER	No, don't! Or we'll be just like the animals they've treated us like for months.
PUPIL 4	Years.
PUPIL 3	Exactly.
RINGLEADER	But you're right, everything has changed, and I think that's a good thing. Don't you?

Some agreement from the group; others are less sure.

RINGLEADER	So, we will come up with a plan, but for now we just carry on.
PUPIL 8	Excuse me …
RINGLEADER	Yes?
PUPIL 8	We want to know …
RINGLEADER	Know what?
PUPIL 8	…what did you do with them?
RINGLEADER	Oh. *Them*.

The Ringleader throws a knowing look to a couple of the pupils.

The fewer of us that know, the better. Trust me, if you don't know what happened, you can't be blamed for it, can you? Agreed?

PUPIL 8	I guess.
RINGLEADER	Right. So, you and you …

To Pupils 8 and 9.

… sort out food, find out what we've got and how long it'll last. You are in charge of the offices; I think someone with a track record

305

310

315

320

15

	for arson should know what to do with all $\quad$ 325 of our official records.
PUPIL 6	Cool – and I can pick the locks on the filing cabinets!
RINGLEADER	(*smiles*) Perfect. Now, you two go to the storeroom and make sure that our … $\quad$ 330

Seems to be thinking of the right word.

… our 'stock' is secure.

PUPIL 2	'Stock.' Like it.
PUPIL 3	On our way.

They exit.

RINGLEADER	And you, you're in charge of … of fresh water.
PUPIL 5	(*confused*) Eh? $\quad$ 335
RINGLEADER	(*clearly speaking in some sort of code*) *Fresh water.*
PUPIL 5	But, we've got loads of…

Suddenly realising.

Oh, right. OK. I'm on it!

Exits.

RINGLEADER	And you lot, clean up this place – it's a mess. 340
PUPIL 10	(*insistent*) No way!
RINGLEADER	(*suddenly angry*) This is not a place without rules! It is a place with new rules! I will have order!
PUPIL 9	Right, OK, understood. $\quad$ 345
RINGLEADER	(*calming*) Good. Oh yes – I have one request. I want your names.

PUPIL **10**   Our names? What do you mean?

RINGLEADER   That's one thing that they always used against
                us – they wouldn't call us by our first   350
                names, like human beings. Well now, I want
                to take your names, your first names, your
                personal names, your nicknames. I want
                to reclaim them and put them to use.

PUPIL **7**   I haven't got a clue what you're talking about. 355

RINGLEADER   Our names have only ever been on our files,
                our documents. I'm … freeing them up.

PUPIL **7**   Are you going to put them up in lights?

RINGLEADER   Oh, it will be better than that, trust me.
                But they're not mine to take – they're   360
                yours to give. So, will you all give me your
                names?

A murmur of confused approval.

RINGLEADER   Good, thank you. I hope you like what I do
                with your name, *in your name*. This is day
                one, year zero, new regime, clean slate. Now 365
                we are all equal – but I'm in charge. So go to
                your jobs, and the rest of you, keep a lookout.

They exit.

Scene 4

The Island voices are spread around the stage.

ISLAND VOICES **3**   And the lookouts looked out, and they
                        saw parts of the old place in a new
                        light – brighter faces. A lightness in the air. 370

ISLAND VOICE 2	And in others, they saw that the old fear remained, that people talked quietly in corners. Furtive, restless.
ISLAND VOICE 4	And they heard the difference too, with none of the familiar squeak of staff trainers on 375 highly polished tiles. Just the gentle slap, slap, slap of the pupils' flip-flops.
ISLAND VOICES	Because you can't run away in flip-flops.
ISLAND VOICE 1	And the absence of the sound of keys on chains. 380
ISLAND VOICE 5	And through the day, a quiet descended, as people got on with what was asked of them, or what they chose to do.
SAM	It's strange to think that I'll be the one who's free from this place before you. It's not the 385 usual way out, I'm sure you'll agree, but it's the one which seems to make most sense to me. In truth, it's the only one I can see. I could have tried to stay longer but it would only have been prolonging the 390 inevitable, so I have decided to get it over and done with.
ISLAND VOICES	And the lookouts looked out.
ISLAND VOICE 4	Nothing.
ISLAND VOICE 5	Nothing. 395
ISLAND VOICE 3	Nothing.
ISLAND VOICE 2	Something?
ISLAND VOICE 1	What something?
ISLAND VOICE 6	Something over there?
ISLAND VOICE 3	In the water. 400

ISLAND VOICE **2**	A boat.
ISLAND VOICE **1**	Small boat or big boat?
ISLAND VOICE **2**	Small boat.
ISLAND VOICE **6**	People?
ISLAND VOICE **3**	Two.
ISLAND VOICE **1**	Police?
ISLAND VOICE **5**	Don't think so.
ISLAND VOICE **1**	Officials?
ISLAND VOICE **4**	Think so.
ISLAND VOICE **6**	From the company?
ISLAND VOICE **2**	Don't think so.
ISLAND VOICE **3**	Word travels fast for such a large place.
ISLAND VOICE **5**	Along the corridors, the slap of flip-flops on bare feet.
ISLAND VOICES	Hard to run in flip-flops.
ISLAND VOICE **1**	Through the halls.
ISLAND VOICES	Very undignified, flip-flops.
ISLAND VOICE **5**	Down the stairs to the dining hall.
ISLAND VOICE **4**	Which is fast becoming the hub.
ISLAND VOICES	The HQ.

405

410

415

420

Pupils and Ringleader gather quickly on-stage to hear the report back from the beach.

PUPIL **1**	(*concerned*) One small boat – two people, official looking, just landing.
RINGLEADER	(*calmly*) Good.
PUPIL **1**	Good?!

RINGLEADER	Yes; like I said, a plan will emerge, and one 425 is emerging.
PUPIL 3	And what does this plan look like?
RINGLEADER	It's a bit vague at the moment, but I'll let you know when it firms up.
PUPIL 2	So for now? 430
RINGLEADER	For now, everything as normal.
PUPIL 2	Normal?
RINGLEADER	Normal-ish. Someone needs to go and greet them.

Looks at Pupil 1.

You've got, how should I put it, *good people* 435
skills …

PUPIL 1	Thank you very much.
RINGLEADER	… so you do that. Someone needs to *secure their boat*, if you know what I mean.
PUPIL 4	I know exactly what you mean, and I know 440 just the place.
RINGLEADER	You, relieve them of *any burdens*.
PUPIL 5	(*smiles*) No problem.
RINGLEADER	And then we'll … play it by ear. After all, we don't even know who they are yet. 445 They might be accountants for all we know.

They exit.

SAM	Thanks to all of you for your special little gifts. I know it sounded odd. Me asking for such a strange thing, but still it was all 450

you ever had to give; they're not big on
possessions in this place are they – and each
and every one of them large and small
served a purpose. The look on some of
your faces was a bit odd; no doubt you   455
were wondering what my 'special project' was
going to be. Now that you know, I wonder
how many of you were surprised. I think
a few of you knew what I had in mind; I
know there are others who have shared   460
the same idea.

*The Island voices gather as if looking at the
beach from the windows of the building, as the
Inspector and Assistant enter.*

ISLAND VOICE 5	And down on the beach …	
ISLAND VOICE 6	… the little boat pulled in …	
ISLAND VOICE 3	… engine off …	
ISLAND VOICE 1	… uneasy quiet …	465
ISLAND VOICE 2	… just the lap of the waves …	
ISLAND VOICES	… Shh … Shh … Shh …	
ISLAND VOICE 4	… they stand, the two figures …	
ISLAND VOICE 5	… with damp feet …	
ISLAND VOICES	… looking at the building.	470

*The Inspector stands as if looking up at an
imposing structure.*

INSPECTOR	Fantastic place.
ASSISTANT	Looks just like in that promotional thing.
INSPECTOR	Well it would, wouldn't it?

*Pupils 1, 4 and 5 enter, at first unseen by the
Inspector and Assistant.*

PUPIL 1	Hi! Can I help you?
INSPECTOR	(*surprised*) Oh, hello. Well I do hope so. 475
ISLAND VOICES 1, 2 AND 3	Pleasantries exchanged, but uncomfortably.
ISLAND VOICES 4, 5 AND 6	And up at the house, the faces watch from the windows.
PUPIL 1	(*with an air of relief*) So … you're from the Educational Inspectorate? 480
INSPECTOR	(*slightly baffled*) That's right.
PUPIL 1	That must be such interesting work. And you're here to …?
INSPECTOR	Just to have a look around. Nothing serious. We have never actually visited before, you 485 see. There's obviously been some problem with the communications.
PUPIL 1	(*mock surprise*) Has there? Really?
INSPECTOR	Yes, very unusual for everything to go down – landlines, email, mobiles … 490 everything.
PUPIL 1	Oh … yes, of course. There was a problem – last night – but it's OK now.
PUPIL 4	Like you said, 'nothing serious'.
INSPECTOR	Good. Well we thought we'd make sure 495 everything was all right.
ASSISTANT	(*as if asking for a name*) And you are?
PUPIL 1	(*evasively*) I am … here to show you round. And how long will you be with us?

INSPECTOR	Just as long as it takes to get the feel of the 500 place.
PUPIL 1	Right.
ISLAND VOICES	Shh … Shh … Shh …
INSPECTOR	Should we follow you then?
PUPIL 1	Yes, sorry, of course, what am I thinking? 505
PUPIL 4	I'll make sure your boat is safe.
INSPECTOR	Much appreciated.
PUPIL 4	No problem. Leave it to me.
PUPIL 5	And please, let me take your coats and briefcases and things. 510

They pass them across.

ASSISTANT	Thank you very much.
PUPIL 5	(*smirks*) My pleasure. Believe me.
PUPIL 1	So, let's have a look round then shall we?
INSPECTOR	Yes, let's.

They walk a circuit of the stage, watched by all Pupils.

ISLAND VOICES 1, 2 AND 3	As the figures from the beach approach 515 the big house …
ISLAND VOICES 4, 5 AND 6	… the faces at the windows look on in horror.
ISLAND VOICES	With each approaching step the tension rises.
PUPIL 9	Oh no. This is bad. Very bad. 520
PUPIL 10	Who are they?

The Ringleader strides on and addresses all Pupils and Island voices clearly and authoritatively.

RINGLEADER   It's OK, there is no need to panic. This will
             be fine; we just need to play it carefully so,
             for now, tell yourselves 'it's just a normal
             day'. Go to where you *should* be, where   525
             you *would* be if this were a normal day.
             OK? And calm … make it look good, like
             everything is fine and the place is running
             smoothly. Go!

             They all scatter to do as they are told as the
             Inspector, Assistant and Pupils arrive, centre.

Scene 5

We see the Inspector and Assistant being
shown round by Pupil 1 as we hear more from
the promotional DVD. For each section of the
Principal's speech the Pupils and Island voices
illustrate the activity as the Inspector and
Assistant look on.

PRINCIPAL   At Hope Springs, and at every Youth   530
            Correction Limited facility, we look after your
            child for twenty-four hours a day, seven days
            a week. From the moment they get up their
            day is structured, managed and controlled.

            Regimented, regulated movements of Pupils
            moving round the site, all Pupils looking
            strangely content. The Inspector and Assistant
            nod approvingly and move on to another activity.

            Education consists of a comprehensive set 535
            of instructive and interesting audio and
            visual presentations to which students are

exposed four times a day. After completing
each set of learning experiences, pupils are
tested and examined on what they have   540
learnt. If successful, they move on to a
higher level; if not, they simply start again.
It is therefore in your child's interests to
pay attention, learn and progress through
our educational programme.   545

*In unison the Pupils open books, read, take
notes, etc. Again the Inspector and Assistant
move on to see another part of the facility.*

The board and staff of Youth Correction
Limited believe that a healthy body, a
healthy mind and a healthy attitude are
all interconnected. Physical Instruction is
therefore a daily priority for all of our   550
young people.

*A regimented exercise regime is displayed. The
Inspector and Assistant move on again, but this
time the Inspector should look more quizzical,
troubled.*

Of course, no young person can spend
their whole day learning and taking part in
an exercise regime – and that's where our
Family Meetings comes in. Family Meetings 555
are our pupils' chance to gather socially
and our chance to discuss important
issues with them. We like to feel this is
where we are able to impart and encourage
a set of values and a moral code to these   560
young people.

The family meeting is shown as a circle of chairs
where everyone mimes talking animatedly and
happily.

We aim to set a guiding framework in minds
which have seen far too little structure; it's
a chance to foster self-discipline and offer a
guiding hand and, yes, perhaps a shoulder   565
to cry on.

On this final move the Inspector and Assistant join
a table of Pupils as they mechanically but happily
eat. They too are given food, which they eat. The
Assistant seems very pleased, but the Inspector is
showing signs of being distinctly unnerved.

Dietary requirements at our facility are
maintained to the highest standards. There
is no choice of junk food here, as there is
simply no choice. Each day the same   570
balanced and nutritious meal is provided.
Perhaps this is not as exciting as a range
of meals to choose from, but this is not
a holiday camp, and they can have all
the choice they need when they leave us   575
and return to you as well-balanced, self-
disciplined young adults.

At the end of the presentation the Island voices
peel away from the other Pupils and watch the
action from a distance.

Scene 6

The Inspector and Assistant are polishing off
their lunch, as are many of the Pupils. The

*Inspector pushes away a bowl and addresses
the Pupils gathered. The Ringleader is hanging
back, merely observing.*

INSPECTOR   Well that was … very … I must thank you
for showing me round; it's certainly been
an eye opener. Very instructive. That has   580
helped me a lot. I don't think there's much
else I need to know … except – *where
are the staff*?

ASSISTANT   (*as if suddenly realising*) Oh yes.

*There is a silence. All eyes slowly fall on the
Ringleader.*

RINGLEADER   And then you go and spoil it all by saying   585
something stupid like …

ASSISTANT   (*to one of the Pupils*) Where *are* the staff?

RINGLEADER   (*stares at the Assistant and approaches*) You
know those moments when you just
want to turn the clock back – just by a   590
minute – to have the chance to start again.
This is one of those. I so wish you hadn't
asked that. I so wish you could un-ask
that question.

INSPECTOR   Really?   595

RINGLEADER   (*looks at Inspector*) Really, really.

INSPECTOR   So what's the answer?

RINGLEADER   Can't tell you.

INSPECTOR   What is going on here?

RINGLEADER   Nothing.   600

INSPECTOR   Nothing?

RINGLEADER	Nothing much – you can see that everything is fine.
INSPECTOR	Everything *looks* fine.
RINGLEADER	Exactly.	605
INSPECTOR	But it's not fine – is it? Where are the staff?
PUPIL 2	(*stepping forward, smiling*) It's a … a training day.

As the Pupils begin to tease the Inspector and Assistant, there is regular laughter from the other Pupils.

ASSISTANT	Oh, there you are then.
INSPECTOR	I don't think so.	610
PUPIL 2	They have them every now and then.
INSPECTOR	Training?
PUPIL 2	Training.
INSPECTOR	And they just leave you to your own devices? That doesn't seem to make sense to me.	615
ASSISTANT	(*hopefully*) They might.
PUPIL 2	(*with no attempt to really convince*) It's part of that whole 'fostering self-discipline' thing, you know. Life skills.
ASSISTANT	(*as if it has all been explained*) Right!	620
PUPIL 3	(*stepping forward*) They're not training.
INSPECTOR	So?
PUPIL 3	(*with mock shock*) They're on strike – they didn't like the regime here, didn't want to carry on, so they went out on strike, just walked out, in protest.	625

INSPECTOR	All of them?
PUPIL 3	All of them … just walked out.
INSPECTOR	Even the principal?
PUPIL 5	Haven't you heard? We're the bad kids, we 630 don't have principles.
RINGLEADER	Yes even our glorious leader, the principal, is gone.
PUPIL 1	They're not on strike.
INSPECTOR	Really? 635
PUPIL 1	They're …

With sudden mock concern.

… not well. A virus. All taken off the island.

INSPECTOR	(*attempting to exert authority*) Look, this is serious – and I would advise you to take it seriously. Something has happened. I need 640 to know what it is, and then I need to do something about it.
RINGLEADER	And what, exactly, are you going to do?
INSPECTOR	I will call the mainland and get someone from the company over there to sort this out. 645
RINGLEADER	But you know that all the communications are down.
INSPECTOR	Then I will simply use my …

*Looks for phone, but finally sees Pupil 5 holding
it up.*

RINGLEADER	I don't think so.

*The Assistant does the same, but sees Pupil 5
holding it up too.*

INSPECTOR	Then we will have to leave ...	650
RINGLEADER	On?	
ASSISTANT	The boat.	
INSPECTOR	(*realising*) Which isn't where we left it, is it?	
RINGLEADER	Oh no.	
ASSISTANT	I can look for it.	655
RINGLEADER	Please do.	
PUPIL 4	But don't forget we know every inch of this island. While you're looking for it at point A, we'll be moving it from point B to point C, and when you get to point B, it'll be back at the first place you looked.	660
RINGLEADER	And we wouldn't want you to get lost – would we?	
ASSISTANT	No. No, we wouldn't.	
INSPECTOR	You're not stupid are you?	665
RINGLEADER	Mad, bad and dangerous to know ... but not stupid.	
ASSISTANT	What's going on here?	
RINGLEADER	I'm sorry to say you picked about the worst time possible to drop in on our ... happy home.	670
PUPIL 7	Last night would have been worse.	
RINGLEADER	(*nods*) True. But still, let's just say, you're way out of your depth. Welcome to 'Hope Sinks'. You really have no idea what you've stumbled into, have you?	675
ASSISTANT	We've seen a sort of, promotional film, about the place. It looked ... OK.	

RINGLEADER	The public face, the marketing?
ASSISTANT	Yes. 680
RINGLEADER	(*mockingly*) You think you *know* this place because you've seen its publicity?
ASSISTANT	Well I …
RINGLEADER	You have no idea! This place is about control. Control and fear and humiliation. Cold and 685 businesslike. Very businesslike. And all paid for by our loving parents, and all profits to the shareholders.
INSPECTOR	Look, whatever has happened here, it's time to put a stop to it now. It will only get 690 worse – worse for you, all of you. Now listen, what's your name by the way?
RINGLEADER	Me? I don't have it right now – someone else is … using it.
PUPIL 5	(*laughing*) 'Using it' … that's right. 695
INSPECTOR	You don't have a name?
PUPIL 3	None of us do. We gave them away.

The Inspector appeals to the rest of the Pupils, none of whom offer any help.

INSPECTOR	I think it would be better for you, all of you, if we did this my way.
RINGLEADER	*Your way? All* ways here are *my* ways. This 700 island's mine!
INSPECTOR	What I'm trying to say is that you wouldn't want to do anything unwise.
RINGLEADER	(*with a laugh*) Are you some kind of eternal optimist? 705

INSPECTOR	Meaning?
RINGLEADER	Meaning, you are surrounded by people who, according to their parents, have been doing 'unwise' things for years. That's why we are here, isn't it? But something makes 710 you think we're going to draw the line on doing *unwise* things … at you? You hope!

Scene 7

PUPIL 7	(*to a nearby Pupil*) I didn't do anything unwise; never had the chance!

Steps forward and addresses the group.

I had mates who were doing unwise things 715 all the time – mad stuff I didn't even want to try. But it was them doing it, not me. But that wasn't good enough for my parents … oh no! I used to sit upstairs and listen to them … 720

Each Parent enters as they speak.

PUPIL 7 AND	(*sarcastically*) What is happening to our child?
PARENT 1	(*earnestly*) We used to talk. Now it's just come home, slam the door and up to the bedroom. I blame those friends … 725

Pupils freeze as the Parents play out the scene.

PARENT 2	But I still think that what you're suggesting is …
PARENT 1	Is what?
PARENT 2	Is a little extreme.

PARENT 1	You think so?	730

PARENT 2   Yes.

PARENT 1   But it's an extreme world, isn't it? To make
any difference you have to fight fire with
fire. It's not like when we were young. If we
want to call ourselves loving parents, we   735
need to do something.

PARENT 2   As far as I can see, we've got a normal
teenager …

PARENT 1   Who is hanging round with abnormal ones,
who are into who knows what! You can   740
close your eyes and hope for the best, you
always do, but I am not prepared to take
that risk …

*Parents 1 and 2 freeze in their final position as
the Pupils re-animate.*

PUPIL 7   But I never thought they'd – you know – really
do it.   745

PUPIL 8   (*steps forward*) Mine seemed to think that
I was the devil incarnate. I admit I was
doing some dodgy stuff, but what I love is
this way they have of thinking that every
good trait you have comes from them and   750
every bad one you have comes from the big
bad world. I used to have these full-on
rows …

PUPIL 8 AND   I don't know how you can speak to me like
PARENT 3   that. Don't you know we slaved day and   755
night to give you the best – never a thought
for ourselves – and all we ask in return is
some respect.

Pupils freeze; Parents still talk directly to Pupil 8.

PARENT **4**   You've been pushing your luck for some time
now. I think you know that; I think we all   760
know that. But don't think our patience is
going to last much longer.

PARENT **3**   If you don't buck your ideas up, then
you'll find yourself …

PARENT **4**   Let's just say you are skating on thin ice.   765
Time is running our for you; so think twice,
that's all I'm saying, think twice.

PARENT **3**   One day you'll just find that you've run out
of last chances. You have to think about
what this is like for us; we're worried sick   770
about you …

Parents 3 and 4 freeze, Pupils re-animate.

PUPIL **8**   And the next thing you know – I'm here.

PUPIL **10**   (*steps forward*) Mine were totally split –
one who actually remembered what it was
like to be young and the other was all …   775

PUPIL **10** AND   Well I never did anything like that at that
PARENT **5**   age – and if I had I'd have been in trouble for
it, I can tell you. We're too soft and it
won't do any good in the long run; we
need to nip it in the bud.   780

PARENT **6**   If we send our child to somewhere like that,
we might as well hold up our hands and say
we have failed. The whole point of being
a parent is to be there when things get
tough, not pass the buck to a bunch of …   785

PARENT **5**   What?

PARENT 6	A bunch of … I don't even know what to call them!

PARENT 5 Professionals! – that's what I call them. People who deal with this stuff day in day out – and 790 we don't, do we? You just don't want to spend the money!

PARENT 6 It's a lot of money!

PARENT 5 And our child isn't worth it?

PARENT 6 That's not what I'm saying!   795

PARENT 5 It sounds like it.

Parents 1, 2, 3 and 4 re-animate, and join in the debate.

PARENTS 2 AND 6 Does it ever occur to you that our child, our own flesh and blood, might hate us forever if we do …?

PARENTS 1, 3, But might thank us forever, too, for not   800
4 AND 5 sitting back and doing nothing.

They exit in two camps, as if at the end of an argument. The Pupils re-animate.

PUPIL 10 And the next thing you know, I'm bundled into a car on the way home from town. No warning, nothing. I thought I was going to die. I thought I was being kidnapped.   805

PUPIL 3 You were.

PUPIL 6 They came and got me from my bedroom at night.

PUPIL 7 They pretended I was going on a trip.

PUPIL 3 Some trip.   810

PUPIL 7 Yeah – some trip.

35

INSPECTOR	Whatever feelings you have towards your parents – you can't take that out on the staff here. It's not their fault; they're just doing a job.

815

RINGLEADER	(*as if a raw nerve has been touched*) Just doing a job?
INSPECTOR	That's right. And if you're keeping them somewhere against their will, then …
RINGLEADER	Do I look like the kind of person who would do a thing like that?

820

INSPECTOR	I have no idea.
RINGLEADER	Exactly – scary isn't it.
INSPECTOR	No.
ASSISTANT	(*almost involuntarily*) Yes.

825

Scene 8

RINGLEADER	Now, you have to believe me, I am as sorry as I can be that you're here. It's not exactly part of my grand plan, not that I really had one. But please, do not think you can come here and tell us what we should and shouldn't have done to the poor hard-working staff of this noble institution.

830

PUPIL 5	Yeah, they're lucky that we didn't …
RINGLEADER	(*spins round to look at Pupil 5*) Stop.
PUPIL 5	Sorry.

835

RINGLEADER	You might be right – they were just doing their job. But anyone who could do that job should expect some …

INSPECTOR	Retribution?	
RINGLEADER	No.	840
INSPECTOR	Revenge?	
RINGLEADER	(*annoyed*) No! It was 'redress', a balancing of the books. You see, from the moment we were taken from our beds, bundled into cars, grabbed from the street, it starts. The programme.	845
PUPIL 3	The programme.	
INSPECTOR	The programme?	
RINGLEADER	The programme dictates every moment of our lives.	850
PUPIL 1	Everything we do.	
PUPIL 2	Everything we eat.	
PUPIL 4	Everything we say.	
PUPIL 5	Every place we go.	
PUPIL 3	Everything we see.	855
RINGLEADER	But the best trick, the really classy touch, is that the programme controls everything we think.	
PUPIL 3	Tries to.	

As they speak, the Ringleader walks to a chair placed centre.

RINGLEADER	Yes, tries to. Good point, tries to. And it's straight in, no messing. Day one. No gentle introduction.	860

The Ringleader is now both in the dining hall and in the introductory interview. The Staff enter

*and stand at the shoulder of the Ringleader. The
Principal enters.*

PRINCIPAL   This may come as a shock to you, but your
parents care enough about you to send you
here; they trusted us enough to let us try   865
to help you.

RINGLEADER   Is that right?

PRINCIPAL   That's right. But they, and we, can't do
this alone. One way or another, sooner or
later, you will work with us.   870

RINGLEADER   I don't think so.

PRINCIPAL   You don't want to know how many, just like
you, I've heard say that.

RINGLEADER   (*angrily*) You're right – I don't.

PRINCIPAL   (*calmly*) You can resist if you want, but   875
you will stay longer. Unless you, as I say,
'work with us', we might well have the
pleasure of your company in the facility,
on the programme, until the day of your
eighteenth birthday.   880

*The Inspector, Assistant and Pupils are watching
the scene unfold.*

INSPECTOR   And then?

PUPIL 6   And then we're adults, legally, and we can
walk right out of here.

RINGLEADER   Will I get a cake?

*The Principal speaks the next section almost
without thinking. It has clearly been said many
times before.*

PRINCIPAL   You will do as you are told, when you are   885
             told, where you are told. You will progress
             only by earning the right to progress. You
             begin at the bottom, at Level 1, and you rise
             through the programme earning privileges.
             At present you have precisely none. No   890
             privileges.

RINGLEADER   Which means?

PRINCIPAL   (*not in answer to the question, but as
             continuing part of the rehearsed speech*) On
             Level 1, students are forbidden to speak,
             stand up, sit down or move without   895
             permission. When you have earned enough
             points to reach Level 2, you may speak
             without permission. On Level 3, you are
             granted a staff-monitored phone call home.
             Levels 4, 5 and 6 will offer you considerably 900
             more privileges; you get to wear some of
             your own clothes, have some snacks of
             your own, play some music of your choice.

             *The Principal begins to use a more usual tone as
             the speech ends.*

             And every student is free to leave when they
             have progressed through the levels and   905
             are proud to say to us, the staff, that the
             programme has 'saved … their … life'.
             That's all. No big deal. But I don't think
             we'll be there for some time yet.

RINGLEADER   I think you might be right—   910

PRINCIPAL   (*angrily*) Stop! I did not ask you to speak. Until
             I do, you say nothing.

INSPECTOR	(*slightly horrified*) Is this true?	
PUPIL **10**	Oh yes.	
PUPIL **6**	All of us got the same … welcome.	915
PUPIL **8**	I sat there for ages.	
PUPIL **6**	With me, the principal got on with other stuff. I thought I'd been forgotten about, didn't know what was going on.	
PUPIL **10**	It's all a game, you see. Eventually though, the instruction came.	920
PRINCIPAL	(*calmly*) Speak.	
RINGLEADER	Well … It seems to me that someone in my position – someone on Level 1 – has nothing to lose; I have no privileges, so there's nothing you can take away.	925
PUPIL **10**	(*looks at Inspector*) That's what we all thought.	
PRINCIPAL	You'd think so wouldn't you? But where would we be then? How would we … progress? Now that is where O.P. comes in.	930
STAFF **1** AND **2**	O.P.! Assume the position!	

All Pupils apart from the Ringleader get into 'O.P.'. Assistant looks shocked.

Scene 9

INSPECTOR	O.P.?	
RINGLEADER AND PRINCIPAL	'Observational Placement.'	
RINGLEADER	Otherwise known as lying on your face, arms by your sides on a tiled floor, taken	935

there by force if necessary, and watched
over, by people just doing their jobs. Fifty
minutes in every hour.

ASSISTANT   And then you get up?   940

RINGLEADER   Just for the ten minutes.

INSPECTOR   And then?

RINGLEADER   Back down, all day. You get some kind of basic
meal at some point, then you sleep on the
bare floor until dawn – when it all starts   945
again.

INSPECTOR   Another day of it?

RINGLEADER   At the start of the next day, you get reviewed
by staff and if you show – I love this phrase –
'sincere and unconditional contrition',   950
then you get out, but if you're still angry,
rebellious or defiant …

INSPECTOR   (*finds it hard to believe*) It carries on?

*As they speak, the Pupils stand up from the O.P.
position.*

PUPIL 5   I spent six months in O.P.

PUPIL 6   I know of a girl who was in it, on and off,   955
for eighteen months … Some people have
a stubborn streak.

PUPIL 8   No matter what level you're on, what privileges
you have, being sent to O.P. takes you back
to Level 1.   960

PUPIL 9   Zero privileges.

PUPIL 6   It's a powerful tool.

PUPIL 7   You're not kidding.

PUPIL **6**   Makes you think twice.

RINGLEADER   But administered by people who were …   965

Sarcastically.

… just doing their jobs.

INSPECTOR   Right, I see.

All Pupils still on the ground rise. There is an unspoken threat in the air.

RINGLEADER   That's why some of us bear a grudge. There's
a strange kind of peace when it's just you, no
sound, no distractions.   970

ISLAND VOICES   Shh … Shh …

RINGLEADER   (*calmly and intently*) Eventually, you hear
the strangest things – your own heartbeat,
and the sound of your breath and
the blood in your veins. Some people   975
say you can even hear your own nerve
endings firing if you've been in there
for long enough. It's a good place to get
thinking done, a good place to plan ahead,
a good place to work your hate into a   980
fine, sharp point.

Controlling, but revealing a rage within.

For me the time in O.P. was like putting
deposits of hatred into a bank account,
little by little, until I was rich in hatred. And
last night I made a massive withdrawal,   985
cleared out my account, spent it all in one
go, like you do. Blow it all on 'something
unwise'.

Indicates the Pupils.

Others chipped in of course, emptied out
their accounts too. There was a lot of hatred 990
and bitterness, a lot of resentment stored up.

PUPIL **10** Months of it.

PUPIL **5** Years of it.

RINGLEADER (*comes in close to the Inspector*) That's why I had
to kill the staff, all of them, and used a bit 995
of each and every one of them in our meal.
Seemed right somehow. Four and twenty
blackbirds, baked in a pie. Did you enjoy it?

*There is a mix of response from the Pupils, some
horrified, some disbelieving, some very calm or
even relishing the moment.*

INSPECTOR (*calmly*) I don't think that's true, is it?

ISLAND VOICES Shh … Shh … 1000

*There is a stillness, centre stage. The rest of the
acting space comes alive as the Principal and
Parents emerge, taking up their places from the
opening.*

SAM I'm not good with words, and this letter isn't
saying half of what I want to tell you
all – so you'll have to imagine what I mean.

PRINCIPAL *So, when things look bleak, when you are at
the end of your tether …* 1005

ALL PARENTS We were at our wits end.

SAM I'm not particularly optimistic about
what is in store for me, but there's always a
chance I'll see you on the other side.

PRINCIPAL	*Remember – there is a way forward. It's* 1010 *not hopeless …*
ALL PARENTS	What else were we supposed to do?
SAM	At least I'll be free of this place, out of their reach, a place of safety… . Goodbye.
PRINCIPAL	*… just when you think there's nowhere* 1015 *to turn – Hope Springs.*

Act Two

Scene 1

*On far parts of the stage a few Pupils lounge,
relaxed. Centre stage, the Inspector sits thinking
while the Assistant paces, panicked. The Island
voices look on, unseen.*

ISLAND VOICE 3   Late afternoon in the Hope Springs
Correctional and Educational Facility.

ISLAND VOICE 1   A calm has descended on the building …

ISLAND VOICE 2   … people simply getting on with what they
need, or want, to do.   5

ISLAND VOICE 5   In the dining hall, two figures …

ISLAND VOICE 4   … not knowing quite what they should, or
can, do.

ASSISTANT   I said it!

INSPECTOR   You said what?   10

ASSISTANT   'Can't the police go …?' Those were my exact
words. I said: 'Can't the police go …?'

INSPECTOR   I know, I remember.

ASSISTANT   'It's hardly a matter for the police,' you said!
Well if this isn't, I don't know what is.   15

INSPECTOR   Keep calm.

ASSISTANT   (*panicking*) People have been killed!

INSPECTOR   They have not been ki—

ASSISTANT   They have! They said!

INSPECTOR   What they said and what they did are two   20
different things.

ASSISTANT	You hope!
INSPECTOR	I'm sure.
ASSISTANT	(*stops pacing, looks around*) But did you see the looks on the faces of the other ones? 25 They seem to think it's true. They seem to think they're capable of it.
INSPECTOR	Which doesn't *make it* true, I was looking at their faces, the ones who claim to have done it – they didn't look like killers 30 to me.
ASSISTANT	Oh, and you're the expert?
INSPECTOR	No, I'm just saying …
ASSISTANT	'Can't the police go …?' I said it. 'It's a bit of a grey area,' you said. We are not cut out for 35 this.
INSPECTOR	There are factions here though, divisions – we can use that.
ASSISTANT	(*sits facing the Inspector*) Factions?
INSPECTOR	Yes. Some obviously approve 40 wholeheartedly of whatever has happened, but those others are … are not so sure; they have that look of not wanting to be blamed for something they had no part in.
ASSISTANT	They look scared. 45
INSPECTOR	They were scared before; now they're scared again.
ASSISTANT	Yes, they've just changed who they are scared of – some liberation that is.
INSPECTOR	Some of them must have been close on 50 getting out of here, must have been model

pupils, done what was needed to get
through the programme.

ASSISTANT   (*exasperated*) And how, exactly, do we *use* that?

INSPECTOR   If you were to take some time, and just talk   55
to them. Find out which ones just wanted
to keep their heads down and get out as
soon as possible – they might talk.

ASSISTANT   (*shakes head*) They'll be too scared.

INSPECTOR   Perhaps if you offer something?   60

ASSISTANT   And what do I have to offer?

INSPECTOR   You can say that, when this is all over, we will
speak up for them, say they helped us to
put things right. They won't be implicated.

ASSISTANT   I can't offer that, I don't have any say …   65

INSPECTOR   Just tell them we'll do our best for anyone
who helps us to clear up this … this mess.

ASSISTANT   And what if those others find out? What
happens to me then, eh?

INSPECTOR   That, I am afraid to say, I do not have an   70
answer for.

ASSISTANT   Right … thanks.

INSPECTOR   But our options, I think you will agree, are a
little limited.

Scene 2

*A group of Pupils enter with brooms, dustpan
and brush, etc.*

PUPIL **9**   Excuse me, we need to clean up a bit in   75
here. Do you mind moving?

INSPECTOR	I thought you were in charge. Aren't you supposed to *tell* me what to do?
PUPIL 9	I suppose so.
INSPECTOR	Go on then.
PUPIL 9	Move … please.
INSPECTOR	My pleasure.

The Pupils begin to clean up the space.

ASSISTANT	If I ran this place now, like you do, I wouldn't waste my time clearing up; I'd be in bed.
PUPIL 10	(*grudgingly*) There's still stuff to be done, apparently.
ASSISTANT	There are still rules then?
PUPIL 10	Oh, yeah, there's still lots of rules.
ASSISTANT	Seems to me like nothing's changed then.
PUPIL 9	(*seriously*) Everything changed, last night. Everything.
INSPECTOR	Why last night? What happened last night?
PUPIL 9	(*looks around at the others*) I don't think I should say.
INSPECTOR	Why not?
PUPIL 10	Just trust me – it's different, OK? Not like before.
INSPECTOR	What happened to the staff? Where are they?
PUPIL 10	You heard what they said.
ASSISTANT	Do you think that's true?
PUPIL 10	I don't know, do I?
PUPIL 8	I do. I bet they did.

80

85

90

95

100

PUPIL 9	It's not true. They wouldn't.
PUPIL 7	They would.
PUPIL 8	Not normally. 105
PUPIL 6	But after last night …
INSPECTOR	Last night?
PUPIL 6	That was the spark …
PUPIL 10	It's very easy to get very angry very quickly in this place. 110
PUPIL 6	This place has been waiting to go up for ages. It just needed a spark.
INSPECTOR	Go on.
PUPIL 10	They try and break you. Everything's controlled and ordered – not even allowed 115 to go to the toilet unsupervised. They manipulate you.
PUPIL 8	Even the way you speak and think.
PUPIL 10	The groups they break us into are called 'families'. 120
PUPIL 7	Some weird kind of family that is.
PUPIL 10	And each family is called something stupid like 'Dignity' or 'Wisdom'.
INSPECTOR	There's nothing stupid about Dignity.
PUPIL 10	But there isn't any, that's what I mean. It's 125 not exactly dignified to have to put your hand up to go to the toilet – but with either one or two fingers raised.
ASSISTANT	Depending on what you need to … to go *for*?
PUPIL 8	Exactly. Dignity? I don't think so. 130

PUPIL 10	And the staff, the heads of the 'families', you have to call them 'Mother' or 'Father'.
PUPIL 6	That's sick that is.
PUPIL 10	I wouldn't do it … well, not to start with.
ASSISTANT	So?
PUPIL 10	Straight into O.P.; soon brings you round.
PUPIL 6	And there's no free time, no time to just be … you.
INSPECTOR	What about your 'Family Meetings'?
PUPIL 10	Oh, they're a whole different sort of torture.
PUPIL 7	They mess with your head.
PUPIL 10	It's not just about modifying behaviour and self-discipline; that's part of it – but really, they're trying to re-programme us, rewire our brains. Learn to think the way they want us to.
PUPIL 9	But …
PUPIL 10	'But' what?
PUPIL 9	… if you're honest, your not telling the *whole story* though, are you?
PUPIL 10	(*sarcastic*) Oh here we go.
INSPECTOR	(*looks at Pupil 9, then Pupil 10, then back again*) What do you mean?
PUPIL 9	They all talk like they're these poor little kids who never did anything wrong, but we're not here for no reason are we? We aren't saints are we? There's something, something that each and everyone of has

135

140

145

150

155

done which our parents were worried
about, worried sick about – but none of you
ever put yourselves in their place do you?   160

PUPIL 10   They've really worked their magic on you
           haven't they.

INSPECTOR   Maybe there is a point there, though.

PUPIL 9   None of them are brave enough to say it –
           but we're here because of our own actions,   165
           something we've done. I am.

INSPECTOR   In what way?

PUPIL 9   (*almost blurting it out*) I was argumentative,
           disrespectful, I was smoking, drinking,
           staying out and going to places where it   170
           was wiser to keep my distance – and my
           parents put a stop to that, because they
           cared.

PUPIL 10   (*angry*) Because they couldn't cope with
           you, and they bought their way out of   175
           dealing with you.

PUPIL 9   I was on course to leave this place, I was
           doing well …

PUPIL 10   You were playing the game!

PUPIL 7   The game, yeah.   180

PUPIL 9   I was progressing through the programme; I
           was on my way to being at home, back with
           my parents …

PUPIL 10   The parents who sent you here!

PUPIL 9   Yes, the parents who want the best for me.   185
           And I worked hard to get that far!

PUPIL 10   Oh, we all know how you've worked. We've all
seen you at work, and don't they love you!

STAFF 1   (*calling out*) Family meeting!

Scene 3

*Staff 1 and 2 enter briskly Pupil 9 and others
begin to congregate for the meeting. Pupil 10
is still outside of it, talking to the Inspector and
Assistant. For the first time, Sam joins the action
instead of sitting outside of it. (Note: depending
on gender, the staff member should occasionally
be called 'Father' or 'Mother'.)*

PUPIL 10   The programme is designed to let them   190
get into your head. It's like a war – if you
pretend to be just going along with it to
gain credits, then they'll sniff it out. And
you'll go back for it.

STAFF 1   Right – who'd like to start?   195

PUPIL 8   No thanks, not me.

PUPIL 7   Not me.

PUPIL 9   I'd like to.

PUPIL 10   And they turn us all against each other. We
can all progress through the programme   200
by telling on others – we actually work for
them; it's the ideal stitch-up.

PUPIL 9   But, well I'm sorry, but I don't think we are all
here yet.

STAFF 1   Good point, thank you.   205

PUPIL 10	There's no trust among us – they kill all that, so we're all out for ourselves.
PUPIL 9	And this isn't the first time this has happened.
STAFF 2	I've noted that, thank you.

To Pupil 10.

I think we have addressed the issue of your 210
tardiness before haven't we? I am talking
to you …

Pupil 10 joins the family meeting.

PUPIL 10	(*to staff 2*) Yes we have.
STAFF 2	But it never seems to get any better, does it?
PUPIL 10	I feel it's getting a bit better. 215
STAFF 1	But there's still that resentment there isn't there – that bad attitude.
PUPIL 10	I think my attitude has improved; I am trying.
STAFF 1	(*looks around the group*) Are we convinced?

*An unsure murmur from the Pupils – some 'yes',
some 'no'.*

STAFF 2	Right, now we can make a proper start. 220 You were saying?
PUPIL 9	I'd like to start by saying that I feel I've reached some kind of a landmark.
STAFF 2	(*looks interested*) In what way?
PUPIL 9	My call home, the last one. Well it was better, 225 much better. Each time I call I can feel the anger – because I admit I was angry – gets less and less. I feel like I know what it

must have been like for them a bit now.
Like I can put myself in their shoes.   230

STAFF 1 Does anybody else feel like that?

More murmuring.

STAFF 1 We've had this conversation before, haven't
we – about trying to see things through your
parents' eyes. How are you doing with it?

SAM Me?   235

STAFF 1 Yes.

SAM OK, it's going OK.

STAFF 2 Meaning?

SAM I'm trying, but, if I'm honest, I find it hard.

STAFF 1 Could you imagine, if you were a parent,   240
sending your child here in the future.

SAM I won't have children.

STAFF 2 That's not what was asked.

SAM But if I'm never planning to have kids,
then there's no point asking …   245

STAFF 1 There's every point.

PUPIL 9 That's not what you were saying the other day.

SAM What did I say? I didn't say anything – I don't
think I did.

PUPIL 9 You said that if you ever had kids you   250
wouldn't send them to a place like this, I
remember that.

PUPIL 10 You remember that, do you?

PUPIL 9 Yes, actually I do.

PUPIL 10 How convenient, *actually*.   255

PUPIL 7	(*laughing*) Actually.
STAFF 1	Attitude!
SAM	I did say it. I was very upset!
STAFF 2	What about?
SAM	What about? This! Being here. 260
STAFF 1	More specifically?
SAM	There isn't a specific – it's the whole thing. I am finding it, sometimes, hard to not be upset. I don't suppose that's unusual is it?
STAFF 2	It's not unusual, but we need to manage 265 it, address it, channel it.
SAM	I *do* manage it.
STAFF 1	How.
SAM	I calm myself down; it's OK. I manage to do it; it's fine. 270
PUPIL 9	I know how you 'calm yourself down' – you want us all to feel so sorry for you. Like it's any harder here for you than the rest of us.
STAFF 1	Meaning?
PUPIL 9	Ahh. Meaning … that it is hard in here for 275 all of us, but we can choose to make it easier on ourselves. And if it wasn't hard it wouldn't work, would it? It wouldn't help us.
STAFF 1	Good. I like your answer. Nice and honest.
PUPIL 10	You're kidding! 280
STAFF 1	Watch it!
PUPIL 10	(*holds up hands*) OK!
STAFF 2	(*to Sam*) But you – it still sounds to me like you're being evasive, devious.

SAM	I'm not, I'm being honest – we're supposed 285 to be honest in these sessions.
STAFF 1	But telling us you'll never have children so you don't need to think about sending them here, that wasn't open and honest was it?
SAM	But I won't ever have kids. It's a fact. 290 Honestly, I wasn't lying!
STAFF 2	This is not about lying …
SAM	(*exasperated*) But it is, it is!
STAFF 2	No.
SAM	It is! It is about lying; the whole thing, all of 295 this, is held together by lies.
STAFF 2	Stop.
PUPIL 10	(*to Sam*) Don't.
STAFF 1	You – keep out of this!
SAM	You lie to us about trying to help us, we 300 lie to you about believing your lie, and we all lie to our parents about understanding their position.
PUPIL 9	I'm not lying!
STAFF 2	(*to Sam*) Stop. 305
SAM	And we lie about each other to make our lives easier, and if I tell you the truth I get into trouble and if I lie it's OK. I just don't get it.
STAFF 1	*One more word* and you're on O.P.!
	The Island voices are outside the scene, as if voicing the thoughts of the Pupils.
ISLAND VOICES	Shh … Shh … 310

All the Pupils look to Sam, trying to urge silence.
A pause.

SAM   (*a decisive, sudden outburst*) And you must
      lie to yourself …

BOTH STAFF   O.P.!

The Staff begin to grapple with Sam. Through
the next speech, some Pupils look on
impotently; others look away.

SAM   … that's all I can think. You lie to yourself
      that you are helping us, but you know the   315
      truth; you lie to yourself so you can do this
      day in day out and sleep at night and take
      the money! There, that's the truth, so
      what's my reward? I don't know how you
      sleep at night, and I've told you, I have   320
      been honest, which I was brought up by my
      parents to be, so what do I get for that? What
      do I get for that?

Sam is taken forcefully from the scene as the
speech ends. A silence.

PUPIL 8   Unwise. Very unwise.

Scene 4

Returning to the present, the Pupils resume
cleaning the room. Pupil 9 suddenly feels as if
accusing eyes are watching.

PUPIL 9   Don't look at me like that. I didn't want to   325
          come here any more than anyone else,
          and yes I played along to get out, but the

hardest thing for you to grasp is that they actually have a point …

PUPIL 10   What?   330

PUPIL 9   … that for some of us, it *works*.

PUPIL 10   You're mad.

PUPIL 9   For some of us this, all this, the whole thing, is *exactly* what we needed!

PUPIL 8   Stop it – don't argue!   335

PUPIL 10   Like I said …

With contempt.

… they loved you.

PUPIL 9   Whatever you think – I *have* developed self-respect, self-discipline; I *have* a sense of personal responsibility, a desire to do   340
better in future – that's what I was here for, that's what I have worked for, and that's why I was almost out! But now …?

INSPECTOR   (*aside, to Assistant*) That's the one to go for.

PUPIL 10   Now what?   345

PUPIL 9   Who knows?

PUPIL 7   Yeah, who knows?

Ringleader and other Pupils enter. There is an obvious atmosphere.

RINGLEADER   Have I missed something?

INSPECTOR   We we're just talking.

ASSISTANT   It's all right to talk isn't it?   350

RINGLEADER   Of course.

PUPIL 9   I'm going for a walk – if I may.

RINGLEADER	Up to you. Good isn't it?
PUPIL 9	(*flatly*) Oh, it's great, yeah.

Exits.

ASSISTANT	I think I'll get some fresh air too. If I may …	355

Begins to leave.

RINGLEADER	You look …
ASSISTANT	(*stops*) What?
RINGLEADER	… scared.
ASSISTANT	(*awkwardly*) Do I?
RINGLEADER	Now why would that be? 360
ASSISTANT	I'm …

Unconvincingly.

… claustrophobic.

RINGLEADER	And that's why you want 'to get some fresh air'?
ASSISTANT	Yes. 365
RINGLEADER	Fine by me.
ASSISTANT	Good, right, OK then …

Exits. The Ringleader fixes the Inspector with a stare.

INSPECTOR	Might I ask, what happens now?
RINGLEADER	(*walking around the Inspector*) I know what you are doing. 370
INSPECTOR	Do you?
RINGLEADER	And if I were you, I'd be doing it to, so it's OK.
INSPECTOR	And what am I doing?

| RINGLEADER | Exposing and exploiting weaknesses, chinks in the armour … | 375 |

Stops.

You're not stupid either, are you?

| INSPECTOR | I don't think so. I hope not. Look, you do realise that fairly soon, if I don't come back, then there will be others. Perhaps tonight, or at the very latest tomorrow. You must have known this couldn't last. | 380 |

| RINGLEADER | It was never meant to last. |

| INSPECTOR | What has it all been about then? |

| RINGLEADER | Something had to give. Breaking point, you know? | 385 |

| INSPECTOR | Because? If I know what happened – maybe I can help. |

| RINGLEADER | You're here to help are you? |

| INSPECTOR | *What happened?* |

There is some kind of unspoken, collective decision to tell the story of the previous evening

| RINGLEADER | This place is designed to break us. | 390 |

| PUPIL 3 | It's what it's here for. |

| PUPIL 2 | And for most people 'break' just means 'wear down', 'pull into line', you know? |

| PUPIL 1 | But some people are special – delicate. |

| PUPIL 3 | Some people almost seem like they're only half there, almost transparent. | 395 |

| PUPIL 4 | They don't have the firm grip on the world that the rest of us have. |

PUPIL 5	Don't have the fight in them.
PUPIL 4	Some people just feel it more than others, 400 don't they?
PUPIL 1	And for those people, 'break' means 'destroy', 'eliminate'.
PUPIL 3	There was one more of us until yesterday – one who was worth more than 405 any of us, was nicer, kinder than us, was a better person, more decent, more honest.
RINGLEADER	Sam.
PUPIL 5	Sam didn't know how to play the game.
PUPIL 2	Didn't know how to knuckle down and lie 410 the big lie.
PUPIL 3	A sensitive soul won't last long here.
PUPIL 1	So yesterday, this sensitive soul got up from their bare bunk, and decided to take control of the only part of their life left 415 to them.
RINGLEADER	The end of it.

Sam wanders unseen through the action.

SAM	I've decided I want a little gift from everybody in the whole place – and I know you don't have anything to give, so … I'd like a 420 pebble from each of you.
INSPECTOR	A pebble?
SAM	Or a stone. Doesn't matter how big or how small. It would be nice if they were pretty, though. 425
PUPIL 1	Mine was pretty.

PUPIL 4	Mine was black with a white line all the way through it.
INSPECTOR	What were they for?
SAM	I can't tell you, but you'll see – it's a … yes, 430 it's a 'special project', that's what I'll call it.
PUPIL 1	One of the things we learn in this place is how to be useful with a needle and thread.
PUPIL 4	'Life skills' they call it.
PUPIL 2	So we can mend our own uniforms. 435
PUPIL 3	When that lonely figure walked off the beach into the water …
PUPIL 5	… they did it with their pockets full of stones – one from each of us.
PUPIL 3	And the pockets all sewn up tight, so there 440 was no danger of any falling out.
INSPECTOR	Why?
RINGLEADER	More weight.
PUPIL 1	Come back here to a night on O.P? Sam didn't want to risk it. 445
RINGLEADER	The uniform was *exposed* at low tide, caught on a rock. Snagged – for us all to see.
PUPIL 4	Where's the dignity in that?
RINGLEADER	*That's* what happened last night. That's when I … when some of us … snapped, 450 as it were.
PUPIL 2	I knew, well I … I had a suspicion what this 'special project' was going to be; well I wasn't sure, so I found the smallest pebble I could. 455

RINGLEADER	I knew *exactly* what was going to happen, so I found the biggest one I could.
PUPIL 2	(*looks at ringleader*) Eh? That's …that's sick.
RINGLEADER	'More weight', that's what I kept thinking, 'more weight'. But at least it was beautiful. 460
PUPIL 2	(*shakes head*) I don't get you.
RINGLEADER	I was looking into the face of someone who wanted to disappear, to be gone, completely gone, for the misery to end. I was asked for help; I helped. 465
PUPIL 3	We were all responsible.
RINGLEADER	It started off like a normal evening, roll-call. But guess what – no Sam. And then the letter, so after that … and then, well – all hell broke loose. 470

Noise of disturbance off stage. Staff 1 and 2 walk on, but remain apart from the story being told. They speak straight out to the audience.

STAFF 1	Excuse me, just what do you think you're doing in here?
PUPIL 5	I think we were quite reserved, considering.
STAFF 2	Right, you are in such deep trouble.
PUPIL 3	They didn't get anything they didn't deserve. 475
STAFF 1	Now, now, come on – don't be hasty.
PUPIL 5	Many times over.
STAFF 2	I mean it; don't do anything you might regret. Think about it.
PUPIL 2	If you ask me, they were lucky. 480
STAFF 1	Please don't, no, please … no.

RINGLEADER   I think we 'channelled our feelings' rather
             well.

             Staff 1 and 2 exit.

INSPECTOR   And the body?

PUPIL 2   Who knows?   485

RINGLEADER   Out there – somewhere.

             *A pensive silence is broken, awkwardly, by the
             Inspector laughing.*

PUPIL 8   Unwise …very unwise.

             *A few of the Pupils move slowly and menacingly
             towards the Inspector.*

INSPECTOR   (*holds out a hand to stop them*) I'm sorry. But
             you really don't see it, do you?

RINGLEADER   See what?   490

INSPECTOR   It's the oldest trick – very simple, very
             effective. And it worked perfectly.

PUPIL 5   What are you saying?

INSPECTOR   You've done all this for nothing.

PUPIL 2   For nothing?   495

INSPECTOR   All this – for a fake, a pretence.

PUPIL 6   A fake?

INSPECTOR   This Sam of yours …

PUPIL 5   Yes?

INSPECTOR   Is still out there somewhere, in hiding, or   500
             has got off the island.

PUPIL 2   There's a letter, to all of us.

The Ringleader holds out the letter, which the Inspector looks at.

INSPECTOR And I thought you were bright. Think. Just think. No one is going to search for a runaway if they've been lead to believe that they're 505 looking for a body, now are they?

RINGLEADER Sam wouldn't do that.

PUPIL 1 The uniform, we found it in the sea …

INSPECTOR But not on the body. Explain that.

RINGLEADER It might have … 510

Unable to think of a reason.

… I don't know.

INSPECTOR Seems odd – to me.

PUPIL 8 What have we done?

PUPIL 7 We should have known.

INSPECTOR This Sam might well have swum for it after 515 leaving some convenient clues – a letter, the uniform. A false trail.

RINGLEADER No!

PUPIL 5 Have you seen how far it is, even to the nearest island? 520

PUPIL 4 No one has done it before.

PUPIL 6 No one has tried before.

PUPIL 10 Sam might have got some sort boat together or something.

RINGLEADER (*angrily but concerned too*) Sam would have 525 told me – Sam is out there somewhere in that water, this is ridiculous.

INSPECTOR   It's a fake. I'm afraid your precious Sam has made a fool of you. All of you.

A pause. Sombre uncomfortable faces all round. The silence is broken by laughter from the Ringleader.

INSPECTOR   Something funny?   530

RINGLEADER   You nearly had me then. But you don't really believe that. Sam's not the fake – you are! You're good. Nice try.

PUPIL **5**   What … what's going on?

RINGLEADER   If you convince them it was all for nothing,   535 then you have the upper hand, you gain control. We knew Sam; you didn't. Last night was no fake.

INSPECTOR   (*looking at the letter*) Wait a minute?

PUPIL **8**   What?   540

RINGLEADER   (*looks at the other pupils*) Don't listen.

PUPIL **7**   What?

RINGLEADER   It's lies.

INSPECTOR   It's even worse.

Looking through the letter.

This was to fool the Staff, the Principal – not   545 you. The clues are there – you were supposed to know it was all a sham.

RINGLEADER   What?

INSPECTOR   (*reading from the letter*) '… *It's not the usual way out, I'm sure you'll agree … I think a*   550 *few of you knew what I had in mind; I know there are others who have shared the same idea.'* It's talking about escape – not suicide.

RINGLEADER   That doesn't prove anything! That could mean …   555

INSPECTOR   Or *'I'm not particularly optimistic about what is in store for me, but there's always a chance I'll see you on the other side.'* Now, why would Sam 'see you on the other side'?

PUPIL **8**   That's true.   560

RINGLEADER   It's not true – none of it.

Appeals to the Pupils.

It's just to break us up, to test our nerve. You're so used to lies that you'll just keep swallowing them. But this …

Grabs the letter and holds it out to the Pupils.

… this is real, this is true.   565

INSPECTOR   Well, if you're sure.

Looking around at the Pupils.

Though I don't think everyone is as convinced as you.

The Ringleader looks at the rest of the Pupils trying to gauge who is still 'on-side'. Suddenly, the Assistant emerges with Pupil 9.

ASSISTANT   We've found them.

INSPECTOR   The staff?   570

ASSISTANT   They're in one of the basement rooms, some kind of store room. They're freezing, they look terrified.

INSPECTOR	They are … unharmed?	
ASSISTANT	I think so.	575
INSPECTOR	Bring them up here; we'll get them warm and fed. I am in charge now, OK?	
ASSISTANT	(*shakes head*) They won't come out.	
INSPECTOR	(*confused*) Won't come out?	
ASSISTANT	They say they feel safer where they are.	580
INSPECTOR	OK, get some food and blankets down there for them. Are they all accounted for?	
ASSISTANT	Not all. All the staff are there, but they …	
INSPECTOR	What?	
ASSISTANT	(*looks uncomfortable*) … they don't know where the principal is.	585
PUPIL 9	(*blurting it out*) They said they saw the principal being carried off.	

The Ringleader looks intently at Pupil 9.

ASSISTANT	Out of the building, into the grounds.	
PUPIL 9	(*more hesitant*) On people's shoulders.	590
ASSISTANT	They weren't sure if the principal was conscious or what.	
PUPIL 9	One said that the principal looked like …	

Is scared to carry on.

INSPECTOR	Like what? What did they say?

Pupil 9 will say no more.

ASSISTANT	They said the principal looked like 'a sacrifice'.	595

The Inspector looks to the Ringleader.

RINGLEADER   Somehow, you suddenly don't look quite so sure of yourself.

INSPECTOR   There's no point in asking, I suppose?

RINGLEADER   The principal has gone to a better place.   600

INSPECTOR   (*angrily*) This is no time to play games.

RINGLEADER   But you're so good at them yourself. You've played with us, but you're forgetting that that's all we learn here – how to play games, to distort the truth, manipulate   605 and control what we can.

INSPECTOR   Not today. Not now.

RINGLEADER   Anyway, you should know where to find our glorious leader.

INSPECTOR   *We* should?   610

RINGLEADER   Of course. If you would just think about it, you'd know. I've as good as told you.

INSPECTOR   I take it the principal will be alive and well?

RINGLEADER   Alive and well? Surely that depends on how quickly you get going doesn't it? I   615 thought you we're in charge – I'm sure I heard you say that.

INSPECTOR   It's very unlikely that anyone would survive another night out in the open.

RINGLEADER   Yes, that's true. So it's over to you now.   620

INSPECTOR   Maybe if you and I just had a chance to …

RINGLEADER   I have so enjoyed our little chat, but don't you have other things to be getting on with?

INSPECTOR   But why can't you just …

RINGLEADER	(*suddenly angry*) Enough – no more! The	625
	principal is in a very special place. If you	
	can't find that place … well that's hardly my	
	fault is it?	
INSPECTOR	But …	
RINGLEADER	As of now you are making me angry – and	630
	you would not like me when I'm angry!	

*A moment at which the Ringleader and Inspector
stare intently at one another. The Inspector
breaks the moment and exits, leaving with the
Assistant and Pupil 9. The Ringleader calmly
sits, centre stage.*

Scene 5

*The Ringleader remains seated centre. Other
Pupils are present but distant.*

ISLAND VOICES	And so the factions fractured. The divisions	
	divided.	
ISLAND VOICES 2 AND 3	With some pupils doing everything they could to help in the search, aware	635
	that each useful act was a credit in their	
	favour, a deposit in the bank of	
	goodwill.	
ISLAND VOICES 1 AND 5	But others simply sat, watched the clouds, watched the waves, skimmed stones, waited,	640
	and stayed silent, keeping what they knew	
	to themselves.	
ISLAND VOICE 4	The hours passed, and the day began to grow	
	dark.	

The Inspector rushes on, clearly anxious.

INSPECTOR   You have to help.   645

RINGLEADER   Do I?

INSPECTOR   Yes. I think you have to.

RINGLEADER   I have helped! You're just not working hard
enough are you? If you were as smart as
you like to think, the principal would be   650
under a blanket by now sipping hot sweet tea.
That's what they give you for shock isn't it?

INSPECTOR   What do you mean you've *helped*?

RINGLEADER   I won't help again.

INSPECTOR   Are you really that bitter? That's sad; you're   655
a bright kid.

RINGLEADER   (*looks away from Inspector*) A bright kid. True.
But bitter too. Intelligent and angry, what
a mix that can be eh? The only problem is,
I'm more angry than I am intelligent – lost   660
sight of what's in my own interests.

INSPECTOR   (*quietly*) You're not like the rest.

RINGLEADER   I take after my father – we're very alike, a
weird mix.

INSPECTOR   Of?   665

RINGLEADER   (*looks at Inspector*) He's a university lecturer,
very high up. I was brought up surrounded
by the classics, twentieth-century literature,
poetry. He's very highly thought of, well
respected, loved by his students and   670
colleagues. Very popular man, my father.

INSPECTOR   Right …?

RINGLEADER	You'd have thought that all that exposure to the great works would give you some sense of what it means to be human wouldn't you – that's what it's all supposed to be about isn't it, all those poems, and novels and plays? All about the business of being a person and how to relate to other people.	675
INSPECTOR	You've lost me.	680
RINGLEADER	You see, none of that knowledge, wisdom, advice and guidance from the world's greatest minds didn't stop my father being what he was at heart.	
INSPECTOR	Which was what?	685
RINGLEADER	Devious, dishonest, manipulative, scheming.	
INSPECTOR	Strange, for such a popular man.	
RINGLEADER	Oh all this was behind closed doors. In the safety and comfort of his own home, my home. Such a nice man in the public eye. So …	690

Pauses to find the right word.

	… abusive in private.	
INSPECTOR	That's a very strong word to use.	
RINGLEADER	And very carefully chosen, believe me.	
INSPECTOR	I see.	695
RINGLEADER	I have gone from one abusive situation to another – because that's what this is, isn't it? You know it is. And he sent me here when I got strong enough to begin to get back at him. You see, that was his downfall – that I'm so like him. I can be everything	700

I've seen him be, everything he taught
me to be. Bright, articulate, charming,
persuasive – but with a vicious streak.
You see, I nearly ruined him, his career, his 705
finances, his standing in the community, all
of those things that mean so much to him; I
nearly took them all away – as payment.

INSPECTOR   For …?

RINGLEADER   His stealing my childhood from me. He   710
took my faith in adults and my ability to live
without fear. He took my dreams of what a
family, what a parent, could be, should be,
and gave me nightmares instead. How do
you repay that? How do you even begin?   715

INSPECTOR   This is not the way!

RINGLEADER   Oh, but it is! This is all part of an ongoing
battle. I've been sent here but my dear
father, but as you said, it won't last, and
I'll be out and back on his case.   720

INSPECTOR   You're not saying that all this, everything that
happened, was just to get you out of here?

RINGLEADER   Oh no. It was a healthy display of anger,
rage and pain. I didn't make this happen.
I didn't start this – *they* did.   725

INSPECTOR   But you *can* end it.

RINGLEADER   And why would I want to do that?

INSPECTOR   To prove to yourself that you're not as like
your father as you think you might be.

RINGLEADER   It's in the genes, hard-wired; I've learnt   730
from a master.

INSPECTOR	Isn't it a pupil's duty to go beyond a master?
RINGLEADER	Oh … very good … very clever.
INSPECTOR	Well?

A pause. It seems the Ringleader might be wavering. The other Pupils emerge from where they have been quietly watching through the last scene.

PUPIL 2	(*urging silence*) No.	735
PUPIL 1	Not now.	
PUPIL 4	Now we've come this far.	
PUPIL 5	(*malevolently*) The principal can rot.	
PUPIL 6	(*looking round for support*) Perhaps we should.	740
PUPIL 8	Maybe it's gone far enough.	
PUPIL 7	Too far.	
RINGLEADER	(*looks at the appealing Pupils, then snaps round to the Inspector*) As I have already told you, the principal has gone to a better place.	
INSPECTOR	Better?	745
RINGLEADER	A very special place, a place where the principal would want to be.	

The Inspector is suddenly struck by something mentioned before; we see an awareness spread. The Principal enters, speaking just as at the opening of the play.

ISLAND VOICES	Play.	
PRINCIPAL	*There are days when being the principal of this institution can be hard. On those days I*	750

*take a few hours to myself and walk to what
I feel is a very special place indeed.*

INSPECTOR   Where are they?

RINGLEADER   (*toying*) Where are what?

ISLAND VOICES   Play.   755

PRINCIPAL   *… nestled deep within the woods, far from
the main house …*

INSPECTOR   Will you show me?

ISLAND VOICES   Play.

PRINCIPAL   *The water that gushes from these rocks at*   760
the mouth of this isolated cave …

ISLAND VOICES   Forward.

PRINCIPAL   *They knew then that they had found a
better place.*

INSPECTOR   If you leave us to search, we may be   765
bringing back a body.

ISLAND VOICES   Play.

PRINCIPAL   *… and here I sit and reflect when I
need to recharge my personal batteries,
before I rejoin the battle …*   770

PRINCIPAL AND   *It's not easy, it's not attractive; our methods*
RINGLEADER   *can, at first, seem excessive, but they are
necessary.*

ISLAND VOICES   (*with alarm and horror*) Stop!

Scene 6

PUPIL 9   Over here, down here, quick!   775

ASSISTANT   Oh no.

The Island voices gather and survey the scene.

ISLAND VOICE 2   The principal looked so different, in the dark
                   of that cave. There was just a candle in
                   there but then, the torchlight – right in the
                   face.   780

ISLAND VOICE 4   Like a … like an animal in car headlights.
                   Barefoot, stumbling around on bare rock in
                   six inches of water.

ISLAND VOICE 1   Freezing water. The feet were blue.

ISLAND VOICE 3   The eyes … so … well, the principal   785
                   certainly hadn't slept the night before …

ISLAND VOICE 5   … maybe not even so much as sat down.

ISLAND VOICE 6   The wrists were bound with that tough
                   nylon rope. And the other end tied right up
                   high. Those wrists looked … pink, raw.   790

ISLAND VOICE 4   You could tell that the principal wasn't sure if
                   we were there to help or to … you know.

ISLAND VOICE 1   And the hands, sore and swollen, gripping
                   onto a stone – like a flint, sharp, cold.

ISLAND VOICE 3   I thought the principal was trying to use it to   795
                   cut through the rope – but when our eyes
                   got used to the light, then we saw them.

ISLAND VOICES   The names …

ISLAND VOICE 5   … carved into the wall of the cave.

ISLAND VOICES   Our names.   800

ISLAND VOICE 4   Scratched in the rock – with that stone.

ISLAND VOICE 6   There was so many of them.

ISLAND VOICE 2   Written everywhere that the principal
                   could reach.

ISLAND VOICES	Every name.	805

ISLAND VOICE 4   Every pupil.

ISLAND VOICES   So many names.

ISLAND VOICE 1   I saw my own name.

ISLAND VOICE 3   And I saw mine.

ISLAND VOICE 6   A punishment meted out *with* my name –   810
in my name.

ISLAND VOICE 5   It was weird, like I was responsible – *but I
didn't do it*. But still there was my
name – the name I had given away.

ISLAND VOICES   I didn't know ...   815

*The Assistant approaches the Principal and
assists with a blanket and a supporting arm. The
Principal is lead towards the centre of the stage.*

RINGLEADER   (*to the Inspector*) You wanted to know my
name? My name is out there now, carved
in stone, by the hands that used to
run this place.

Grabs the Principal's hands.

These hands.   820

Holds the Principal's face.

Don't you forget us now. We won't forget you.

*The Inspector indicates to the Assistant to take
the Principal away. They all watch the Principal
exit with support.*

What can I say – it seemed right somehow.
My name and all the names. A testament,

a document. A proof that this happened and we were here. A monument. A war memorial.   825

INSPECTOR   This war is over.

RINGLEADER   Is it?

A moment of unease. Some look to the floor, some to the Ringleader, some to the Inspector.

INSPECTOR   (*authoritatively*) You – the boat, the boat we came in – get it, now! I want it back, where   830 we arrived, in five minutes. OK?

PUPIL 4   (*looks to the Ringleader, who does not look back*) OK.

INSPECTOR   You! My telephone, here in two minutes! All right?

PUPIL 5   Right.   835

INSPECTOR   (*to the Ringleader*) And you …

The Ringleader approaches, puts a hand in a pocket and pulls out a key.

INSPECTOR   And this is …?

RINGLEADER   The key to the principal's office. Everything else is in there – the keys to every other office, all the computers, phones, faxes –   840 you could want. I suppose you think it's time to tell the world what we've done here.

INSPECTOR   I think we should.

Scene 7

The Island voices slowly place themselves as if creating a boat, which the others take up positions in.

ISLAND VOICES	Shh … Shh … Shh …	845
ISLAND VOICE 6	So the boats came and went that night …	
ISLAND VOICE 5	A flotilla.	
ISLAND VOICE 4	Each with its cargo of huddled blanketed figures.	
ISLAND VOICE 3	The principal.	850
ISLAND VOICE 2	The pupils.	
ISLAND VOICE 1	The staff.	
ISLAND VOICE 2	And on a seat, a still sea-damp uniform.	
ISLAND VOICE 3	The stones still sewn into the pockets.	
ISLAND VOICE 4	Seaweed caught in the buttons.	855
ISLAND VOICE 5	Sand in the seams.	
ISLAND VOICE 6	And it was silent.	
ISLAND VOICE 1	No one spoke.	
ISLAND VOICES	No one new quite what to say.	
ISLAND VOICES 1, 2 AND 3	And on the last boat to leave, still no one spoke, looks were exchanged half-heartedly.	860
ISLAND VOICES 4, 5 AND 6	This was a group of people unsure of what they had done, unsure of what they were going to.	
ISLAND VOICES	Halfway between pride and shame, relish and revulsion, they moved through the night.	865
PUPIL 9	So what are we actually going … to? Where will they take us?	

INSPECTOR	I don't know. There are 'authorities' waiting, that's all I know. 870
PUPIL 3	From the company?
PUPIL 5	The police?
INSPECTOR	To be honest, I don't know.
PUPIL 4	They'll move us somewhere else.
PUPIL 2	They'll separate us. 875
PUPIL 8	They'll go after us for this – they'll have a field day.
PUPIL 10	That's if we're not in prison, youth detention.
PUPIL 1	We've already been in that.
PUPIL 2	Would it be any worse? 880
RINGLEADER	What could they do us for?
INSPECTOR	They might throw in kidnapping, imprisoning someone against their will, there tend to be laws against those kind of things.
RINGLEADER	(*with a smile*) Even on a private island? As 885 part of a business arrangement? A financial agreement? A difficult one to call – legally, I think you'll find it's all a bit of a grey area.
PUPIL 6	And will they really want the bad publicity?
PUPIL 7	Bad publicity – yeah. 890
RINGLEADER	Things like this have a habit of being forgotten – glossed over. Think of those nervous shareholders …
INSPECTOR	Why don't you think of the principal?
RINGLEADER	(*dismissively*) The principal will be fine. A 895 few scratches. A few might even make it to

full blown scars. But it's the nightmares that will last. Still, nothing that can't be survived. Don't they say that 'what doesn't kill you makes you stronger'? So who knows? And 900 we will not be forgotten, which was the point after all.

A pause.

PUPIL **3**   You realise we all should, technically, be back there?

INSPECTOR   (*taken aback*) Because?   905

PUPIL **3**   Remember that first interview, how 'every student is free to leave when they have progressed through the levels and are proud to say to us, the staff, that the programme …'   910

ALL PUPILS   '… has saved their life.'

RINGLEADER   I don't think I can honestly say that, not yet.

INSPECTOR   Unusual circumstances.

RINGLEADER   A bit of a grey area, eh?

ISLAND VOICES   Shh … Shh … Shh …   915

ISLAND VOICES 1 AND **2**   And no more was said.

ISLAND VOICES 3 AND **4**   (*more brightly*) But in one heart, one mind, a decision was reached.

ISLAND VOICES 5 AND **6**   On that boat, unspoken and unnoticed, a corner was turned.   920

ISLAND VOICES 1 AND **2**   Through the pitch of the boat and the night the possibility of a new dawn was embraced.

ISLAND VOICES 5 AND 6 And, as the lights of the mainland came into view, from under the 'grey area' of a blanket … 925

ISLAND VOICES 1 AND 2 … one set of cold hands began to take …

ISLAND VOICES 3 AND 4 … one by one …

ISLAND VOICES 5 AND 6 … the pebbles and stones from their pockets, and let them slip … 930

ISLAND VOICES 3 AND 4 … one by one …

ISLAND VOICES … silently, into the cold black sea.

SAM So, when things look bleak, when you are at the end of your tether, remember – there is a way forward. It's not hopeless; just 935
when you think there's nowhere to turn – Hope Springs.

THE END

QUESTIONS AND ACTIVITIES

Questions

Keeping track

> **Learning outcomes**
>
> You will:
>
> - learn who the main characters are
> - keep track of the main events in the play
> - express your own ideas about the play and its themes.
>
> You will do this by reading the play in class, and stopping at various points to discuss your reaction to the story, the characters and the themes. You will also make brief notes in answer to some questions, and this should help you to 'keep track'.

1   Think about the play's setting. What does the writer tell us about the actors and where they are standing when the play starts on page 3? Do you think the setting for this play is going to be realistic or more stylised and flexible?

2   Now think about the characters. Look through the list at the start of the play (page 1). How many real names are used (e.g. like 'Billy' or 'Jenny')? What does this suggest about the characters in the play?

Copy and complete each spider diagram on page 84, adding any ideas or words connected to the word in the middle.

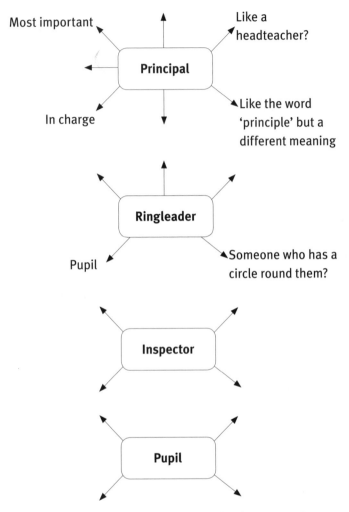

Principal

Most important

Like a headteacher?

In charge

Like the word 'principle' but a different meaning

Ringleader

Pupil

Someone who has a circle round them?

Inspector

Pupil

3   Answer the following questions, which relate to Act One, Scenes 1 to 4.

Staging

* What is the first sound that can be heard as the play opens? What does this suggest about where the play might take place? (In fact, the writer tells us in the bracketed scene direction.)

- The first person who speaks is 'Sam'. What is s/he reading?
- Who 'stands alone', reading what Sam has written?

Different voices

Act One, Scene 1 switches between different voices and situations. First we hear the 'Island voices', then Sam speaks, then we hear the 'Island voices' again.

- The audience is partly watching an advertisement or promotional tape/DVD of 'Hope Springs' when the Principal speaks. Several other people also speak while the Principal explains what 'Hope Springs' is like. Who are they? Are they also on the promotional film?

'Hope Springs'

We find out quite a lot about what 'Hope Springs' is from this first scene.

- Where is it?
- What is it?
- What does it do (according to the Principal)?
- Who is in 'Hope Springs'?
- Is there anything to suggest that 'Hope Springs' isn't quite the same as how the Principal describes it?

The Inspector and the Assistant

- In Act One, Scene 2 we meet the Inspector and the Assistant for the first time. What are they watching?
- What has made the Inspector think they need to check out the 'school'?
- How does the Assistant feel about going to inspect 'Hope Springs'?
- In Act One, Scene 4 they arrive on the Island. What is the Inspector's first reaction?
- Why do you think the Inspector is 'surprised' by who is there to meet them?

The Ringleader

- The Ringleader appears in Act One, Scene 1 reading Sam's letter, but we don't hear from him/her again until Act One, Scene 3. When s/he speaks on page 13, s/he says 'the old rules no longer apply'. What do you think has happened on the Island?
- What evidence is there that the Ringleader is in control of the Pupils, and that they listen when s/he has something to say?
- Later in Scene 3, Pupil 8 asks the Ringleader: '...what did you do with them?' Who is Pupil 8 referring to? Why doesn't the Ringleader tell the Pupils what happened?
- The Ringleader also asks each Pupil to give him/her something. What? Why do you think s/he wants those things?

Island voices

These voices act as narrators or a chorus at various points in the play.

- They are used in Act One, Scene 4 to describe how 'Hope Springs' operates now that the Pupils are in charge (see pages 17–23). What has changed, and what has remained the same?
- Continuing with this scene, who do the Island voices report arriving on the Island?
- Why do you think the writer uses this technique rather than show the arrival itself?

The Pupils

- Of the Pupils, only one has a name – Sam. Sam only speaks briefly at the start of the play, and in the middle of Act One, Scene 4. In the letter s/he wrote (which s/he is reading – see page 20) s/he says thanks to the Pupils for their 'special little gifts'. What do you think s/he was given?

- The Pupils often seem to be like a single mass, but in fact they are all different in attitude and behaviour. In Act One, Scene 3 they are having a discussion. How do Pupils 8 and 9 feel about what has happened?
- What evidence is there that Pupils 3 and 7 feel differently?

4   Now answer these questions, which are about Act One, Scenes 5 to 9.

'Hope Springs': reality and illusion

In Act One, Scene 5 the Pupils attempt to show the Inspector and the Assistant that everything is fine. This is done to the background of the 'promotional' video/DVD we heard at the start.

- What activities do the Inspector and the Assistant see?
- What is the Assistant's response to this?
- How do we know that the Inspector suspects something isn't quite right?
- At the beginning of Act One, Scene 6, the Inspector asks a key question that will force the Ringleader and the others to reveal what has happened. What does s/he ask?
- However, several Pupils come up with lies to hide the truth. How do Pupils 2, 3 and 1 try to cover things up in different ways?

Parents and Pupils

- What had Pupil 7 done to make his/her Parents send him/her to 'Hope Springs'?
- How do Parents 1 and 2 disagree over what should be done?
- Pupil 8 admits s/he was doing 'some dodgy stuff'. What evidence is there that Parents 3 and 4 agree with each other?
- Parents 5 and 6 are even more divided than Parents 1 and 2 over what to do with their child. Why does Parent 6 think they would have 'failed' if they sent their child to 'Hope Springs'? What other argument do they use against it?

The 'Programme'

In Act One, Scene 8 the Ringleader describes what happened once children arrived at 'Hope Springs'.

- Until what age does the Principal say children can be kept in the 'facility'?
- How do Pupils move up from Level 1?
- How do Pupils have to behave at Level 1?
- How does this change as they move up the levels?
- What is O.P.?
- What is the Inspector's reaction to hearing about these things?
- What does the Ringleader say that O.P. (and other treatment) finally led him/her to do to the Staff?
- Does the Inspector believe him/her?

Sam

Sam reappears at the end of Act One reading more of his/her letter. What do you think s/he means by 'I'll see you on the other side'?

5   The next set of questions is about Act Two, Scenes 1 to 3.

The family

- In Act Two, Scene 2 Pupil 10 says that the Pupils were split into groups called 'families'. What sort of names did each family have?
- What did the Pupils have to call the Staff in charge of each 'family'?
- Pupil 10 says the meetings were designed to 're-programme' the Pupils, and make them think in the way the Staff wanted them to. In what way does Pupil 9 disagree with this?
- In the meeting itself Pupil 9 seems quite positive about the programme. What example does s/he give of how s/he has changed?

Sam

- Sam is in the Family Meeting. What evidence is there that s/he doesn't want to speak or explain him/herself?
- What does Sam say about having children?
- Sam says s/he finds it hard to cope and is often 'upset'. Are the other Pupils sympathetic?
- What is Sam's view of 'Hope Springs' and what the other Pupils and Staff say?
- What happens to Sam at the end of Act Two, Scene 3?

6   This final set of questions on the play itself is about Act Two, Scenes 4 to 7.

The Inspector

- In Act Two, Scene 4 the Inspector tells the Assistant to 'go for' Pupil 9 in order to find out what has happened to the Staff. Why does the Inspector choose this particular Pupil?
- What evidence is there that the Ringleader knows what the Inspector is up to?

Sam

- How was Sam different from the others, according to the Pupils?
- What does Sam ask for from each Pupil? What does s/he want them for?
- How did the Ringleader's 'gift' differ from that of Pupil 2? What was the reason behind the Ringleader's choice?

The rebellion

- How does the writer show what happened on stage?
- How do these lines link with the very first scene of the play?
- Why does the Inspector say to the Pupils 'You've done all this for nothing'?
- What evidence does the Inspector offer to support what s/he thinks is the truth about Sam?

The Ringleader

- The Ringleader has been in control for most of the play, but what evidence is there that s/he is beginning to lose grip in Act Two, Scene 4?
- Near the end, we find out quite a lot about the Ringleader's personal history. In what way was the Ringleader's father two different people? What does the Ringleader imply his/her father did? How do you think the Ringleader nearly 'ruined him'?

The Principal and the Staff

- What happened to the Staff?
- What do we learn from Pupil 9 about what happened at first to the Principal?
- Why do they need to find the Principal quickly?
- How does the Inspector finally work out where the Principal is?
- What was the task (the punishment) the Principal had been given to do? Why was this significant?

Leaving the Island

- What does the Inspector say will happen to the Pupils?
- Why does the Ringleader think they might get away with what they have done?
- The play ends with a symbolic act. What is it, and what does it suggest?

What have I learnt?

- How has 'keeping track' helped you to think about the different characters, themes and ideas in the play?
- What have you learned about how you can support your ideas about characters and themes?

ACTIVITIES

Activity 1: The Ringleader

Learning outcomes

You will:

- explore the Ringleader's character
- organise and present your ideas
- make decisions and select evidence to support ideas
- write a short account of your views about the Ringleader.

You will do this by tracing what the Ringleader says and does throughout the play.

1 Copy and complete an enlarged version of the table below.

The Ringleader first appears in Act One, Scene 1 when s/he is reading …
When the Ringleader next appears s/he tells the arguing Pupils that they had to act, even though it was a 'little unwise' because …
The Ringleader asks the Pupils to give him/her …
In Act One, Scene 4 the Ringleader tells the Pupils to behave as if everything is normal because …
The Ringleader organises hiding the boat and taking the Inspector's phone because …
The Ringleader tells the Inspector that s/he didn't want 'retribution' or 'revenge', but 'redress' because …
The Ringleader remembers how s/he was treated by the Principal when s/he first arrived at 'Hope Springs' and how s/he was forced to …
The Ringleader explains to the Inspector how 'O.P.' changed – and also helped (in a way) – him/her by …
The Ringleader tells the Inspector that s/he had to 'kill the Staff'. But we know the Inspector doesn't believe the Ringleader because …

(Continued)

Later, when explaining how 'Hope Springs' drove Sam to act, the Ringleader says that s/he gave Sam the 'biggest' pebble s/he could find because ...

The Ringleader starts to doubt Sam is dead when the Inspector tells him/her that ...

Near the end of the play, the Ringleader explains what his/her father was like and how he was admired at work but at home was ...

At the end of the play the Ringleader finally hands over the key to the Principal's office so the Inspector can ...

2   Compare your responses with others in your class. Then use them to talk about:

- the reasons why the Ringleader leads the 'rebellion'
- whether s/he is defeated or has 'won' by the end of the play
- whether you approve of the Ringleader's actions.

3   By yourself, write a short account of no more than 200 words in which you explain whether you sympathise with the Ringleader. You should quote directly from the play to support the points you make.

What have I learnt?

- What have you learnt about the Ringleader's background before s/he arrived at 'Hope Springs'?
- What have you learnt about this character and how s/he behaves in the play?
- How did selecting material from the text help you to answer a particular question?
- What have you learnt about why it is important to use quotations when writing on a play?

Activity 2: The style and tone of the play

Learning outcomes

You will:

• explore the way a writer creates atmosphere in a play.

You will do this by investigating the opening to the play and writing a short alternative opening.

1   With a partner, re-read the opening scene. Go through it together, then copy and complete this table.

Feature	Page	Details
People who speak who don't have separate characters.	3	*'Island voices'*
Use of voices to create sound effects (not words).		
Use of music.		
Lines that seem to come from another scene or conversation.		
People who speak who have roles/jobs but no names.		
Characters who have names.		
Other type of visual presentation included in what's happening.		
Different people giving different views about 'Hope Springs' and what they feel.		

2   Now join up with another pair and compare your answers. Discuss:
    - why you think the writer has written the opening scene in this way
    - the advantages and disadvantages of this style.

3   By yourself, write a short scene plan that shows the story as it actually happens in ordinary time sequence. Start with the ideas below and add four more scenes.

Scene 1: Parents arguing with their children; Staff taking them away to 'Hope Springs'.

Scene 2: 'Hope Springs' in action – showing how the Pupils are treated.

Scene 3: The arrival of the Ringleader and how s/he is treated.

Scene 4: Sam and the other Pupils having their 'family' sessions.

Scene 5: Sam beginning to ...

Scene 6:

Scene 7:

Scene 8:

Scene 9:

Scene 10: The Principal is freed; the Inspector and the Pupils leave.

What have I learnt?

- What have you learnt about the way the writer has opened the play?
- How did this help you decide whether this was a good opening or not?
- What have you learnt about the order in which things happen in reality and how they can be adapted in plays?

Activity 3: Role-play

Learning outcomes

You will:

- explore a variety of characters from the play
- predict outcomes and explore new ideas
- plan and present your ideas.

You will do this by participating in a role-play that takes place shortly after the play ends.

Imagine that after the play ends, a special inquiry is set up to investigate the events. The inquiry will consist of a judge investigating what happened by questioning various witnesses to get their view of events.

1   In groups, allocate parts for your role-play. You will need to allocate the roles of the Inspector, the Ringleader, the Principal, one member of Staff, Pupil 2 and Pupil 9. A judge (not in the play), played by your teacher, will be conducting the inquiry. The role-play will consist of the judge asking questions and calling witnesses to find out what went on.

2   In your groups, plan and make notes about what you will say in your role-play, which will last between 5 and 10 minutes. Avoid writing out your lines – jot down basic prompts only. You should consider including:

- an account of what happened (the actual events)
- why the Pupils rebelled
- different viewpoints about who was to blame and why
- how the Ringleader and the other Pupils felt about being sent to 'Hope Springs'

- how the rebellion ended
- what people think happened to Sam.

The role-play will end with the judge 'retiring' to consider what action to take.

3   To help you prepare for the role-play, you will need to consider the following questions about your own character.

- How would your character behave in this situation?
  For example, would they be frightened about what might happen to them, or feel bold and ready to stand up to any questions?
- How would your character show their emotions?
  For example, would they pace around nervously or stare at the judge directly?
- How would they speak? Calmly? Or would they hesitate and pause anxiously?

4   Decide how the scene will begin. Will everyone be present? Or will some characters be waiting ready to be called in? Which 'witness' will speak first? Make sure everyone has at least two lines to say.

5   Now, in your groups, you are ready to act out the role-play. Your teacher, in role as the judge, will start the inquiry.

What have I learnt?

- How did performing help you to gain an understanding of the characters and their issues?
- What have you learned about the skills needed in role-play and how good you are at it?
- What have you learned about the relationships between adults and young people and how these work best?

Activity 4: A formal report

Learning outcomes

You will:

- develop analytical skills
- use evidence from the play to present your ideas
- study other texts to understand how they work
- write for a specific audience, with a specific purpose.

You will do this by using details of the play to write a formal report by the judge of the enquiry detailing what happened and what action should be taken. The report will be sent to the Crown Prosecution Service.

1   Meet with your group from **Activity 3** (see page 95) and re-cap on what evidence was heard at the enquiry. Discuss (and make notes on) the following questions.

- If you were the judge, who do you think came out best/worst from the inquiry? Why?
- If you were the judge, what action would you take as a result? (For example, close 'Hope Springs' or send the Ringleader to a proper jail?)

2   Working in pairs, copy down these features from formal reports. Then think about examples for each feature.

- First paragraph **clearly** explains the purpose of the report.
- Language – will be **formal** and **precise**, based on the **information** the judge has been given.
- Useful **organisational connectives** will help to make the report clear.
- Witnesses' words will be in **quotation marks** or will be in **reported speech**.

- The **opinion** of the judge will come **at the end** after **all the evidence** has been considered.
- Decisions or **conclusions** will be backed up by reasons.

3   By yourself, use your notes from **Task 1** to plan and write a formal report for the Crown Prosecution Service from the judge of the inquiry. Include the evidence given by the Ringleader, Inspector, Principal, Staff, and Pupils 2 and 9. End with your recommendation for what action should be taken. If possible, produce your final version on computer. Are there any ways you could make it look more like a real report, e.g. by using a memo-style format, with room for a title, who the report is going to and the date.

What have I learnt?

- What have you learned about the way a formal report is written?
- What skills did you need to plan and write your formal report?

Activity 5: The Principal

Learning outcomes

You will:

- explore the character of the Principal
- organise and present your ideas.

You will do this by exploring how the writer presents the character of the Principal, and write a short account in which you decide whether you agree with how s/he was treated by the Ringleader.

1   In threes, read through the following scenes in which the Principal speaks. Read with as much expression as you can. For example, if the Principal is angry, how will you show this? A different person should read the Principal's words for each scene. The other two can read the remaining parts between them.

- Act One, Scene 1: the Principal's speeches from the video/DVD about 'Hope Springs' (pages 4–9)
- Act One, Scene 5: more speeches from the video/DVD (pages 24–26)
- Act One, Scene 8: the conversation between the Ringleader and the Principal (pages 38–39).

Then, in your threes, look at Act Two, Scene 6 (pages 75–77), which reveals what has happened to the Principal.

2   Now, working in pairs, copy and complete the following table about the Principal.

Scene	What the Principal is doing	Impression given of him/her	Evidence (what s/he, or others, say)
Act One, Scene 1	*Presenting a promotional video of 'Hope Springs' to persuade Parents to send their children to him/her.*		*'Just ask yourself, is your child safer on the streets … or here with us?'*
Act One, Scene 5			
Act One, Scene 8			
Act Two, Scene 6			

Decide from your table whether the evidence you have gathered shows the Principal in a good or bad light.

3   Working on your own, write four paragraphs about the Principal.

- Para 1: write about how the Principal presents 'Hope Springs' and what it offers.
- Para 2: write about the reality of 'Hope Springs' and how Pupils are treated.
- Para 3: write about what happens to the Principal and what s/he is like when found at the end of the play.
- Para 4: write about whether you agree with how the Principal was treated.

Then, returning to your original group of three, share your views and put forward your opinion about the Principal, backed up by evidence.

What have I learnt?

- How has this activity shown you how evidence gathered can be used to draw conclusions about a character?
- What have you learnt about how the playwright presents a major character?
- How did this activity help you to argue your point in your group?

Activity 6: Designing 'Hope Springs'

Learning outcomes

You will:

- explore different ways of staging and presenting the play
- describe and explain your ideas clearly.

You will do this by imagining you are the designer of the play. You will make suggestions to the producer about how the play and characters will look.

1 In pairs, look at Act One, Scene 1. Review how the play's opening shows that it is not a 'naturalistic' setting and style. Consider:

- names and roles of characters
- how the story is told
- use of sound
- anything you think is unusual.

2 In order to create a design for the play, you need to have a clear sense of what it is about (what themes are important, its setting, etc.). In small groups, discuss the following questions.

   a What are the key themes of the play? Consider the following, and talk about how important each one is:

- friendship
- authority
- generation gap
- punishment
- education
- freedom
- depression
- hope

- communication
- power.

b What is the setting of the play, and why is this important? Consider:

- geography (where and what it is)
- what is there
- who is there.

c Who is in the play? Consider:

- whether there are different groups (if so, who)
- the relationship between people (are some people friends, enemies?; are some people in control?)
- how people behave (what they want and what they are trying to achieve).

3 Working on your own, choose **one** of the categories below, then write down your design ideas for your selected category. Explain your ideas clearly and give reasons why you would select the design. You might like to attach drawings or diagrams to your writing.

a How the characters are **dressed**.

- Would you go for a naturalistic feel (e.g. the Principal in a suit; the Inspector with glasses and briefcase)?
- Or would you go for something more unusual (e.g. everyone dressed in black)?

b The **staging**.

- Would you suggest a built set with rocks, water, buildings, etc.?
- Or would you go for something more surreal (e.g. a canvas with video images flickering/changing through the play)?

c **Make-up** or other facial appearance.

- Would you use conventional stage make-up?
- Or would you use make-up to create a particular look or style?
- Or would you perhaps suggest the use of masks?

What have I learnt?

- How does the staging and other design bring out ideas in the play?
- How has this activity taught you what a designer might contribute to a play?

Activity 7: The play's title

Learning outcomes

You will:

- use evidence from the play
- explore themes and ideas
- organise and present your ideas.

You will do this by considering how the play's title links to the themes and action within the play.

1 On your own, copy and complete each spider diagram below, adding any ideas, questions or words connected to both 'Hope' and 'Springs'.

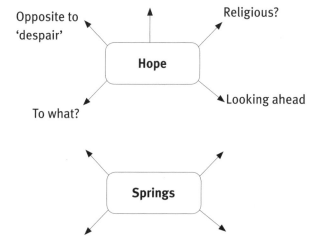

2 In small groups, share your ideas from your brainstorm, then discuss the following questions.

- In what way does 'Hope Springs' have a double meaning in the play?
- What ideas come to mind if you hear of a place called 'Hope Springs'?

- How often – and at what points in the play – is the phrase 'Hope Springs' used? (You will need to scan the play to find where it is mentioned.)
- Why is the location of the cave significant in the story?
- How has your view of 'Hope Springs' changed by the end of the play?

3   By yourself, write the following essay.

Explain why you think Richard Conlon chose the title 'Hope Springs'. How does it draw our attention to the play's themes and ideas? Use evidence and quotations from the play to support your ideas, and draw on the discussions you have had.

What have I learnt?

- What have you learnt about how writers choose the titles of their works?
- What have you learnt about the significance of this title in terms of the play and its ideas?

Activity 8: You, the playwright

Learning outcomes

You will:

- explore new ideas and carefully select one
- write for a specific purpose
- perform for an audience.

You will do this by writing another scene for the play, which you will then perform.

1   A number of other scenes could be added to the play's end. Which of these would be the most interesting?

   a The Inspector gets the chance to visit the Ringleader who is in a new prison just for children and has asked to see him/her. The scene details their conversation and what the Ringleader wants/needs.

   b The Principal has returned to 'Hope Springs' and re-opened it under a new name, 'Calm Horizons'. The scene deals with a time ten years' later when Sam, or the Ringleader, returns (in disguise) for a job interview as a member of Staff.

   c Pupil 3 is sent home to his/her Parents who have heard about what happened. The scene deals with his/her arrival back at the family house.

2   Choose the scene you think would be most interesting, then write your version of it. Think about:

   - the dialogue – check how the characters spoke in the play and make sure how they speak and behave is consistent
   - the stage directions – write these in the same style that Richard Conlon uses

- the need to build your scene to a climax that will work on stage and grip the audience.

3   Perform your scene. You will need to link up with others and divide the roles. Afterwards, reflect on how effective your scene and performance was.

- Was it consistent with how the characters behaved in the play?
- Did the dialogue sound convincing?
- Did it end in an interesting way?

What have I learnt?

- What skills have you used and developed in this activity?
- How is scripting a drama different from other types of story-telling?
- How did it feel to perform in front of others? What were the strengths and weaknesses of your group's performance?